Synchronicity
AND THE
Other
Side

Synchronicity

AND THE

Other
Side

YOUR GUIDE TO

*Meaningful Connections
with the Afterlife*

TRISH MACGREGOR AND ROB MACGREGOR

Avon, Massachusetts

Published by
Adams Media, a division of F+W Media, Inc.
57 Littlefield Street, Avon, MA 02322. U.S.A.
www.adamsmedia.com

ISBN 10: 1-4405-2544-7
ISBN 13: 978-1-4405-2544-5
eISBN 10: 1-4405-2581-1
eISBN 13: 978-1-4405-2581-0

Printed in the United States of America.

10 9 8 7 6 5 4 3 2 1

Library of Congress Cataloging-in-Publication Data
is available from the publisher.

This publication is designed to provide accurate and authoritative information with regard to the subject matter covered. It is sold with the understanding that the publisher is not engaged in rendering legal, accounting, or other professional advice. If legal advice or other expert assistance is required, the services of a competent professional person should be sought.
—From a *Declaration of Principles* jointly adopted by a Committee of the American Bar Association and a Committee of Publishers and Associations

Readers are urged to take all appropriate precautions before undertaking any how-to task. Always read and follow instructions and safety warnings for all tools and materials, and call in a professional if the task stretches your abilities too far. Although every effort has been made to provide the best possible information in this book, neither the publisher nor the author are responsible for accidents, injuries, or damage incurred as a result of tasks undertaken by readers. This book is not a substitute for professional services.

This book is available at quantity discounts for bulk purchases.
For information, please call 1-800-289-0963.

To Don MacGregor 1914–1997
Tony Janeshutz 1913–2005
Rose Marie Janeshutz 1916–2000

ACKNOWLEDGMENTS

Many thanks to Connie Cannon, Jenean Gilstrap, Jeri Gerard, Mike Perry, and the many others who contributed stories. And, as always, a special thank you for our daughter, Megan, for all the joy she adds to our lives.

CONTENTS

INTRODUCTION

Believe it or not, life continues after you die.

While mainstream scientists might say there's no way to prove that contention, that hasn't stopped most people from at least wondering what comes next. Whether you call it the afterlife, the hereafter, life after death, or the other side, it's on our minds from time to time. Some hold to religious beliefs in heaven and hell and are confident that eternity awaits. Others, though, aren't content with faith and want firsthand evidence through personal experience—contact with the other side. If you're one of those people—or think you could become one—this book is for you.

We'll relate numerous fascinating stories of spirit contact, and we'll show how you, too, can make contact. Woven throughout is the theme of synchronicity, or meaningful coincidence, which often plays a role in this exploration. Synchronicity is a connective tissue between the everyday world and the other side, the world of spirit.

The same day we decided to write a proposal for this book, Rob's ninety-nine-year-old second cousin, John, passed away. We know that for a fact, because we searched our e-mail archive and found the note we'd written to the editor of our previous book, *The 7 Secrets of Synchronicity.* The close timing of the two related events—both dealing with the afterlife—was significant, and there was no cause and effect involved, since Rob didn't learn about John's passing for a couple of days. The confluences of coincidental events were meaningful, making it a synchronicity.

Synchronicity and the Hereafter

In Clint Eastwood's movie *Hereafter*, three people are touched by death in different ways. George (Matt Damon) is a blue-collar American who has a special connection to the afterlife, but is not happy about it. Marie (Cecile De France), a French journalist, has a near-death experience that shatters her world-view. And when Marcus, a London schoolboy, loses the person closest to him—his brother—he desperately needs answers. Each character travels a path in search of the truth, and when their lives intersect, they are forever changed by what they believe might—or must—exist in the hereafter.

Granted, Hollywood is not always a loyal reflection of real life, or of death. But Clint Eastwood is a director who does his homework. You can almost see him, a man now in his eighties, motivated by his own mortality, researching life after death and spirit communication with the fervor of someone on a quest. Other writers and directors have gone in the same direction.

In Richard Matheson's brilliant novel (also made into a movie) *What Dreams May Come*, Chris Nielsen (Robin Williams) dies in a car accident, but his consciousness awakens on the other side. He discovers that his wife, Annie (Annabella Sciorra), has committed suicide as a result of his death and is trapped in a kind of hell created by her beliefs. To rescue her, he must enter her reality, a dark, dismal place, a broken-down house.

Such tales, when presented as fiction, are popular, even among those who are skeptical. The truth is that many people have doubts. As Emerson noted in *The Over-Soul:* "The influences of the senses has in most men overpowered the mind to the degree that the walls of space and time have come to look solid, real and insurmountable; and to speak with levity of these limits in the world is the sign of insanity."

As you read on, you'll see that the walls separating this world and the other side are *not* insurmountable, that you can obtain messages from deceased loved ones, that guidance can be found, that a larger picture of life and life hereafter is readily available. In fact, the more contact you make, the more the so-called realm of the dead appears to be buzzing with life, potential, and promise.

The Stories

The stories in this book come from a variety of sources—friends, acquaintances, synchronicity experts, writers, mediums and psychics, and ordinary people who have experienced spirit contact through synchronicity. We include a few of our personal experiences as well. The stories span the spectrum from the relatively mundane (if anything having to do with spirit contact can be mundane!) to the mysterious and the bizarre. You'll discover that Spirit will use just about anything at its disposal to make contact with the living.

When we started blogging in February 2009, we were complete neophytes. The blog was mostly an experiment to see what would happen. We knew we wanted to write about synchronicity, but that it wasn't enough for us to write about just our own experiences. So we created a Google alert for the term and began to sift through countless URLs as they arrived in our mailbox. We dropped by the blogs and websites with posts that addressed synchronicity as Carl Jung defined it—the coming together of inner and outer events in a way that is meaningful to the observer and can't be explained by cause and effect—and gathered stories. Gradually, our community grew and people began to leave comments about their own experiences.

In those two years, the synchronicities in our own lives have multiplied. When you write about this topic, it's impossible to divorce yourself from it. It becomes the fodder of your own life—the stuff that plays out from week to week, day to day and, sometimes, from hour to hour. When spirit contact became part of our synchronicity journey, events began to unfold outside of the laws of cause and effect.

For example, the day after we received an offer to write this book, we headed to Cassadaga, a spiritualist camp in central Florida, a trip that had been planned several weeks earlier to coincide with a book conference in nearby Daytona Beach. With a synchronicity like that, we knew we were on the right track. You'll know it, too. But don't take our word for it. Dive in. Enjoy. Explore.

1

SYNCHRONICITY AND BEYOND

Contact with the other side, the afterlife—imagined or real—often catches you by surprise. It occurs in many different ways, and frequently involves a synchronicity or meaningful coincidence. It can manifest as a voice, a scent, a type of food, a song, a name heard over and over, art, books, animals, clusters of objects or numbers. It can come through a dream, meditation, vision, through a person with mediumistic abilities, or in your everyday life. It occurs during times of crisis and transition, but also during times when your life is humming along at a perfect pitch. Luminaries have experienced it—Carl Jung, Charles Lindbergh, Abraham Lincoln, Mark Twain—as well as people from all walks of life. The essence of spirit contact is overwhelmingly one of benevolence that provides comfort and warning, confirmation, hope, and healing.

Contact occurs most frequently with loved ones who have recently passed on. Sometimes, you may actually glimpse the person you remember or you may hear the individual's voice. But more often than not, the contact is symbolic. Let's say you've been thinking about your mother, who passed away several years ago. You're wondering where she is, what she's doing, who she's with. Or did she simply disappear into oblivion when she died? As if in response to your musings, you suddenly discover one of her best recipes scribbled in her handwriting in a cookbook. Or you smell the scent of her perfume around your home.

Skeptics would dismiss such experiences as mere coincidence, random, meaningless. This kind of experience, however, is a perfect example of how synchronicity and spirit contact work in conjunction with each other. In fact, the most powerful instances of spirit contact usually involve synchronicity.

If you're skeptical about life after death, about spirit contact through dreams or any other means, or even about the importance of dreams generally, it's smart to begin this journey by taking inventory of your own beliefs. Check the statements that apply to you:

❑ I believe in life after death.
❑ I believe that dreams convey all kinds of information.
❑ I have experienced after-death communication through dreams and/or other methods.
❑ I had a near-death experience.
❑ I believe in meaningful coincidence—synchronicity.
❑ I read the signs and symbols in my environment for guidance, direction, and insights.
❑ My spiritual beliefs don't follow any traditional religion.
❑ I am intuitive or psychic.

❑ I have had precognitive dreams or premonitions.

❑ I have received verifiable information through a dream
visitation.

❑ I keep a dream journal and have good recall of my dreams.

❑ I remember some of my past lives.

❑ I have undergone a past-life regression.

❑ I have had a reading with a medium or psychic.

❑ I believe that we are more than our physical bodies.

❑ I feel comfortable talking about my beliefs with others.

❑ I've had an experience with a haunted house.

❑ I meditate regularly.

❑ I am open to all kinds of paranormal experiences.

❑ I consider myself to be a seeker.

If you checked:

15–20: You're a natural for spirit communication. You probably have your own techniques for communicating with spirits
and accurately interpret the synchronicities you experience.
Your intuition is powerful.

10–15: Your experiences with spirit communication occur
when you need confirmation or verification. By nurturing your
intuition, developing it, your experiences will become more
frequent.

5–10: You experience synchronicity and spirit communication from time to time. You may be held back by fear. But fear
of what? Look under the section of this chapter called "The
Modus Operandi of Spirit Contact" for thoughts on dealing
with fears related to spirit contact.

0–5: You rarely experience synchronicity. Possibly, you've
had little or no interest in the subject. But you've picked up
the book. Something within you has changed. Start researching synchronicity. The more you become aware of it, the more

frequently you'll experience it. Start meditating. The practice primes you for spirit communication.

The Other Side of Entertainment

Those of us who experience contact with the other side might confide in close friends or family members, telling them the story. But we're not likely to talk to strangers we meet in a grocery store or on an airplane about it. After all, if you talk freely about contact with the dead, you run the risk of being seen as unbalanced or crazy. Yet, there is a growing acceptance of such encounters in the entertainment world. In fact, contact with the afterlife in television series and movies has become commonplace.

In the popular television series *Dexter*, Dexter Morgan, a police blood-splatter expert who moonlights as a serial killer, frequently holds conversations with his deceased father, who was his mentor. He sees his father so often that he never seems surprised when he shows up. Unlike any of the other characters in the series, the father can't be removed from the show by getting killed. He's already dead.

In the six-year run of the hit TV show *Lost*, characters see dead people so often that viewers soon wonder if they are all ghosts experiencing a mysterious afterlife set on an island. In *Medium*, Allison Dubois works as a consultant for the district attorney's office in Phoenix, Arizona. The premise of the show is based on the reported experiences of a real-life medium by the same name.

The young boy in *The Sixth Sense* sees ghosts everywhere. They speak to him, implore his help, and try to communicate with him. They also terrify him. Perhaps that's one reason why spirits generally choose less threatening means of contact—using synchronicity or subtle signs rather than corporeal appearance to communicate with loved ones.

The deceased even purportedly make appearances on television through the medium John Edward. His program, *Crossing Over*, is particularly intriguing. Edward works a TV audience with the confidence of a politician, bringing messages from the other side.

Then there are the books. Esther Hicks channels Abraham, a group of souls who provide advice and insights on how to live more fulfilling lives. Dannion Brinkley, who has had several near-death experiences, brings messages and predictions from the afterlife. Jane Roberts channeled Seth, a "personality essence no longer focused in physical existence," and together they wrote more than twenty books about the nature of reality.

In the West, we tend to be more skeptical about contact with the afterlife than in Eastern society. Yet, according to a 2005 CBS poll, more than one in five people say they have had contact with someone who has died.

Experiences of Synchronicity and Contact

We've gathered some examples of synchronicities related to contact with the afterlife. Have you experienced any similar ones? How did you feel when they were happening?

- You notice the initials or nickname of a loved one appearing like a doodle on a dusty surface or on a frosty windowpane.
- You keep hearing the same unusual name of a friend who died several years ago.

- During a vacation trip, you notice a bird hanging around, possibly an uncommon one, such as a loon or a raven. A dear friend or spouse who died loved that type of bird, and every year from then on, when you return to the same vacation site, the bird reappears.
- In a dream, a trusted friend or family member who has died tells you to go to the doctor, that you have a health problem that needs attention. Even though you feel fine, you decide to act on the advice and it turns out you're in the early stages of diabetes.
- During your daily meditation, you hear a voice say, "Your father is listening." You open yourself to this possibility and thank your father and mother for all they did for you. The experience is uplifting and confirms your belief that death is not the end.
- You hear your deceased grandfather's voice and glimpse his image in a mirror whenever you're in a crisis.
- Your grandmother was an expert seamstress, and not long after she dies, you begin to find straight pins everywhere. You don't sew. You don't even own any straight pins. They always appear in odd places—on the hood of your car, underlining passages in books, on the floor of a restaurant where you're having dinner. This phenomenon continues for years.
- A dog you've owned for years passes away. Not long afterward, you wake in the middle of the night and hear tapping against the hardwood floor, the same tapping feet you used to hear when your dog was alive. Moments later, you feel a depression at the bottom of your bed, where your dog used to sleep. When you turn on the light, nothing is there.
- You visit a medium, who describes your deceased father and then gives you a message from him that you intuitively know is genuine.

- While traveling, you stay in an old hotel and wake to loud noises during the night. You find that a lamp has fallen over and the television is now on, even though you're sure that you turned it off, and no one else is staying in the room with you. When you mention it to the hotel clerk the next day, she sheepishly admits other people have reported strange occurrences in that room. She thinks it might be haunted.
- You think of a sibling who died, happen to look at a digital clock, and there are the numbers of his or her birth date.
- You inherited a valuable watch from someone close to you, and the watch is frozen at the exact time the person died. Even when the watch is repaired and starts again, it stops at the same time.

Spirits Came Knocking

We've experienced many different forms of spirit contact over the years—sometimes with spirits of people we knew, occasionally with spirits who were complete strangers to us. The contact has run the gamut. Sometimes we nurtured mental and emotional environments that encouraged contact, but just as often, we were minding our own business and the contact simply happened.

Contact with Loved Ones

One winter day in Minneapolis not long after Rob's father died in 1997, his mother, Ione MacGregor, saw the letters M-A-C etched on the frosty window next to the chair in the den where her retired husband spent hours reading each day. Donald MacGregor's nickname was Mac. The incident comforted her. She felt it was her husband communicating with her. It was the first of three incidents of spirit contact with her deceased spouse that became progressively more intense and detailed.

The second incident happened a few weeks later when Ione was in the basement preparing to do laundry. She looked across the room and spotted a glowing orb about the size of a softball in the doorway. It remained visible for several seconds, then disappeared. She felt that the orb was the spirit of her late husband.

Years passed and Ione remained in the family house where she'd lived for five decades. One day in early January, she woke from a nap in the den where she'd been watching television. She looked up and saw Donald standing in the doorway, smiling. She was stunned, because he looked very alive and very much as she remembered him in his later years. The image remained in place long enough for her to look him over and ask a question.

"Where did you get that shirt from?" It was a colorful shirt, as orange as a popsicle. She'd never seen it. He continued smiling, then faded away.

Contact with Strangers

In 2006, while vacationing in the Dominican Republic, we stayed in a hotel on the beach. The hotel consisted of three buildings forming three sides of a square with a "garden" in the middle. When we arrived, we found that the so-called garden was actually a fenced-in graveyard. So our second-floor porch looked out onto the graveyard and the ocean beyond it.

We assumed it was a historical graveyard. One day when the gate was open, we walked in for a look around. We'd barely gone ten feet when we noticed a grave marker indicating the man had been buried four months earlier. He apparently was a windsurfer; his gravestone was the top half of a windsurfing board, and his epitaph read: "Wherever the wind blows I'll be there."

While we were puzzling over the grave, which was about thirty feet from our room, an old man with a shovel approached us. He was digging a grave and was excited because he'd come upon a coffin from an earlier graveyard below this one. He said the sand keeps rising, so graves are stacked one on top of another. He wanted to show us the new grave, but we'd seen enough. As we were about to leave, Rob picked up a smooth stone from the graveyard and took it with him. By this time, our daughter Megan, who was fifteen, was demanding we move somewhere away from the graveyard. We took a three-room apartment in one of the other buildings. Its front porch faced the ocean, but ironically, the entry and side porch had an even better view of the graveyard.

On our last night, we went to bed about 11 P.M. Half an hour later, we woke to the sound of pounding so loud and insistent it seemed to shake the building. BAM-BAM-BAM . . . BAM-BAM-BAM. Three strikes, like a wrecking ball hitting the wall, a pause, three more strikes. After a couple of repetitions, we both bolted upright simultaneously—and the sound instantly stopped.

We'd both heard it. It was no dream. Then we heard voices from inside the apartment. Rob got up and found the television on, even though we turned it off when we went to bed. Megan couldn't have turned it on; she was still asleep in the back bedroom.

The next morning, Rob took the smooth stone and dropped it over the fence into the graveyard. We were the only ones staying in the building, so there was no one to ask about the pounding sound. But, as we checked out, we told the manager what happened. He looked confused, then said, "The spirits here are all friendly . . . *muy simpatico*." Oddly enough, neither one of us had been frightened. We'd actually felt quite energized, as if we'd experienced expanded awareness and contact across dimensions.

This contact was only through sound. We never saw a ghost, but we got the message. We took an interest in the graveyard and the local spirits took an interest in us.

HOW TO REACT TO CONTACT

While there are no hard and fast rules about how to deal with contact, common sense should always prevail.

So let's say you move to an older house, and on your first night you're awakened by the sound of footsteps or a mysterious rapping. Stay calm and look for a mundane explanation. Is a screen loose outside your window? Is the wind blowing hard? Is your six-year-old at your bedroom door?

If you determine that there's no logical cause for the sound, you could be dealing with spirit contact. Take note of how you feel. If you're frightened, anxious, or even annoyed, turn on the light and thank the spirit for stopping by, but say that you don't want to be bothered at night. However, if you're curious or energized, ask the spirit what it wants. You might hear a voice or glimpse an image. Make note of any response and your reaction to the incident.

Chances are the sounds will stop on their own, as the booming sounds did for us in the Dominican Republic. You may even have an inkling about why the experience happened. Be sure to record as many details as you can recall about the experience. If these experiences continue, you might recognize a pattern in your contact experiences.

Physical Evidence

When physical evidence is present, it's difficult to attribute spirit contact to adrenaline or other brain activity, as some psychologists have done. Jeri Gerard recalls an encounter with a lost or trapped spirit in a house where she was living: "It was something very heavy and annoying that wanted my attention. One day, my favorite pen disappeared, a Cross pen, a gift from my mother. I knew that I had left it on the made bed, but it was no longer there. I searched the bed, then the room, then the house. Finally, I turned to the living room and fiercely ordered my pen to be returned. When I went back to the bedroom, it was precisely in the middle of the bed."

In a period of sixteen months, Mike Perry lost three important people in his life: his mother, his closest friend of thirty years, and his daughter. After his mother's death, he and his wife started seeing white feathers everywhere. They also saw them after the loss of his closest friend and daughter. "The odd thing, however, is that they sometimes seemed to almost answer questions," Mike wrote on his blog.

On one occasion, just after his best friend had died, Mike was walking across the square in his town, wondering if his friend was okay. "Out of nowhere, a white feather appeared and fell at my feet. As I continued to walk it flew on ahead and did a sort of big forward circle before falling again at my feet. Perhaps I was clutching at straws but I got an instant feeling inside that things were okay with him and I had no need to worry."

After Mike's daughter died unexpectedly, the same thing happened. One day after visiting her grave, Mike and his wife found a white feather in a glass vase. Now, whenever they find a white feather, his wife exclaims, *"Look! She's thinking of us."*

Such experiences, while not definitive evidence, provide profound reassurance and hope. Anyone who experiences something like this comes away filled with hope that the souls of their loved ones live on.

Your Environment

Your personal environment—at home, at work, any place where you spend a lot of time—influences your openness to synchronicity and to spirit contact. If your family and friends are skeptics, then you may be skeptical as well. If you're a believer surrounded by skeptics, then it's likely you don't share your experiences and beliefs for fear you'll be ridiculed or thought of as odd. If you're on the fence but curious enough to explore, read, and experiment on your own, then your journey, initially, may be lonely.

But once you embark on this journey, you'll begin to attract like-minded individuals. You'll forge new relationships, find new opportunities, and your inner life will be immeasurably enriched.

Do you tend to be a believer, a skeptic, or on the fence? See which of the following descriptions fit you.

Skeptic

It's not unusual to have doubts about the ability to contact the other side. Maybe you even question the existence of life after death. But if you're reading this book, then you are probably interested in the possibilities. Perhaps you've had an experience that you can't explain. Maybe it was a synchronicity that was powerful enough to seize your attention, to prompt you to open this book. Your next step? Learn more. Examine your beliefs about the nature of reality, about life after death.

As your focus on this area intensifies, it may become more difficult for you to withhold your discoveries, thoughts, and feelings from family and friends. If you don't feel comfortable opening up to them, consider starting a blog. It's an excellent way to communicate how you feel, the nuances of your experiences, and what you're learning. Take a workshop in intuitive development or meditation. Sign up for yoga classes. Yoga creates flexibility in both body and mind.

Believer

Since you don't need convincing, you're ready for the next step in this journey. If you haven't already had a reading with a medium, consider trying one. Mediums, by definition, communicate with spirits, so a reading would include messages from a deceased loved one. A reading from a psychic usually involves predictions about upcoming events in your life. Some readers provide a combination of messages from the other side and predictions. You can find more details about readings in Chapter 7.

If you don't meditate already, then start. It's one of the best ways to open your psychic receptivity to spirit contact—and to synchronicity. If you have a meditation practice, then increase the time you meditate and focus on contact with the other side. Take a workshop in meditation. Workshops are helpful for learning various breathing and relaxation techniques that help you to get into the zone more quickly. Foster an environment of belief in your home, office, within your personal circle of family and friends.

On the Fence

When you're on the fence, you're traveling along the border between belief systems. If you take a step to the right or left, gravity takes over. You fall to one side or the other. You're open and receptive, *but*. . . . And it's sometimes a huge *but*, and that's what makes this group the most difficult.

Whether you're a loner or the gregarious, social type, you should seek out groups, workshops, and seminars on synchronicity, reincarnation, life after death, intuitive development, or meditation. Treat yourself to a past-life regression with a qualified therapist. A regression can be enormously revealing, particularly if it takes you between lives. The regression techniques that therapists use are vital in coaxing you into the deeper state of consciousness where information about your past lives is available.

And remember: It's easier to be a cynic than a seeker. A cynic rejects everything without delving into it. A seeker explores, evaluates, experiences, and decides.

A SCIENTIST SPEAKS

Francis Crick, an English molecular biologist, physicist, and neuroscientist, codiscoverer of the structure of the DNA molecule, was dismissive of the afterlife in his book *The Astonishing Hypothesis: The Scientific Search for the Soul.* He thought that if the soul existed, science would know about it. He concluded: "You, your joys and your sorrows, your memories and your ambitions, your sense of personal identity and free will, are in fact no more than the behavior of a vast assembly of nerve cells and their associated molecules."

In Crick's universe, there's no room for believing we're more than our physical beings. Fortunately, that's not the final word. The history of science reveals that science evolves with new evidence. For example, until the nineteenth century, scientists insisted that rocks did not fall from the sky, even though it was a common belief that they did. Now, of course, science accepts the reality of meteorites. But will science ever accept a reality that is invisible to the most advanced electron microscopes and the most powerful telescopes?

For our part, we can't help but wonder what Dr. Crick, who died in 2004, thinks now. Mediums say that nonbelievers enter a dormant state of existence or nonexistence, as their beliefs dictated. But eventually, they realize something astonishing: They exist. From there, anything is possible.

Making Contact

If you're interested in making contact with someone who has died, be sure that you have a definite reason for pursuing the matter. Maybe you want to confirm that life after death exists or that communication with the other side is possible. Or you might want to know if the person you fondly remember is happy. You might also be grieving and hoping that the contact will help you overcome your grief. Be aware that in the aftermath of the contact, you might miss the person even more than you do now. Dealing with grief takes time, and making contact with a deceased loved one isn't necessarily a shortcut to getting over it.

If you want to make the attempt but are afraid, then you need to examine your beliefs. Are they really *your* beliefs or were they imposed on you by another person or persons or through your religious upbringing? Don't attempt to make contact if you have any negative feelings about the process.

Be aware of the limitations of contact. You could have an intense experience with a departed loved one, but the person isn't coming back, at least not as the person you remembered. Also realize that the contact won't continue indefinitely. As time passes, you need to adjust to the new circumstances, let go of the lost loved one, and allow the person to move on. Avoid becoming obsessed with contact. It's better for both of you to recognize that life on earth is for the living.

Being Receptive

If you have a meditation practice, then you know how to enter that state of mind where the rest of the world falls away. Even if you don't meditate, you're probably familiar with that receptive mental state that's open to inner awareness. Some people experience it when they drive, swim, or walk or hike in nature, when they do creative work or yoga, or when they feel deeply relaxed. In any such circumstance, when your mind is open and receptive, you have an opportunity to move into a deeper state of awareness where spirit contact is possible.

The next time you're involved in something you enjoy, think of someone who has passed on, and ask for a sign that indicates spirit contact.

Watch for synchronicities. Maybe you're thinking about the person and hear a song that was once his or her favorite tune, and it's not one that's played very often now. Or you hear the person's name on the radio or television, and it's an uncommon name. Or you glimpse a car that's the same make, model, and color of the unusual vehicle that the person drove. Or maybe when you're feeling the loss strongly, you stumble upon a note or card the person wrote to you long ago. The synchronicity helps reinforce the validity of the experience.

THE LOON OF FOURTH LAKE

Sometimes, as Janice Cutbush discovered, you don't have to request contact to get it—an inner need triggers it. Shortly after Janice's husband, Tom, died suddenly, she visited friends who live on Fourth Lake in the Adirondacks in upstate New York. It was an area where she and Tom used to take the kids every summer. Tom especially loved listening to the loon on the lake early in the morning.

Late one afternoon, Janice went for a swim and suddenly felt a presence near her in the water. She looked up and saw an enormous loon about twenty feet away, all alone. He stayed nearby during her entire swim and left when she got out of the water. Every day of her visit, the loon appeared in front of her friends' home. They began calling him Tom. Her friend pointed out that it was unusual to see a loon alone; they usually travel in pairs and mate for life.

Every year, Janice and her second husband vacation in the area, renting different homes on various lakes. "But no matter where we are, our lone loon appears at some point during the vacation. I like to think it's Tom's spirit visiting us."

Janice's initial experience might never have gone anywhere if she hadn't drawn the connection between Tom's love of loons and the lone loon who landed on the lake. Even though she wasn't specifically asking for spirit contact, Tom's death was still a raw wound, and some part of her needed to know that his soul lived on. So her awareness and receptivity were undoubtedly factors in the experience.

Then there's the synchronistic element—a lone loon landed on the lake as she swam, didn't leave until she got out of the water, and continued to return each day of her visit. The fact that a lone loon still visits, year after year, when she's vacationing in the area, defies the odds. And synchronicity often involves incredible odds.

The Modus Operandi of Spirit Contact

Modus operandi (MO) is a Latin phrase that means "mode of operation." It's used most frequently in police investigations, to signify patterns of behavior, but can be applied to spirit contact as well. Curiously, the MO for the phenomenon of spirit contact is fairly straightforward:

1. The more aware you are of synchronicity, the greater the chances you'll experience spirit contact.
2. If you're open and receptive to the possibility that the soul survives death, then you're nurturing a mental, emotional, and spiritual environment in which spirit contact can occur.
3. Spirits seem to use whatever is available to make contact. Animals and birds, which we cover extensively in Chapter 11, frequently act as spirit messengers. But synchronicities related to objects, foods, music, art, scents, and just about anything else can trigger spirit contact as well.
4. Some people are particularly attuned to spirit contact and experience it frequently. These individuals are generally intuitive and accustomed to using their intuition in their daily lives. Some of them may be mediums or psychics, but neither is a prerequisite. One woman commented on our blog: "I don't usually have waking encounters, only whispers of visits just before I wake. This morning a beautiful woman wearing a complex floral perfume stood next to my bed. Don't know what it means, but it was pleasant."
5. Your beliefs about life after death have a direct bearing on spirit contact. Even if you're open and receptive, you may harbor a hidden fear about spirit contact that could

prevent you from experiencing it. It's best to take a close look at that fear and find its source. Maybe you were frightened by ghost stories as a child and those fears have stayed with you. You might consider visiting a medium, who acts as an intermediary between you and the soul you want to contact. It's best to try someone who is recommended or known for her or his work in the field. The more you learn about it, the less fearful you'll be.

6. Ritual can serve as a vehicle for spirit contact. Many indigenous cultures employ complex rituals that facilitate spirit contact. Among Cuban santeros, spirits are "called" through offerings of foods, rum, sweets, music, and the need and will of the practitioner. In spiritism, an offshoot of spiritualism that's prevalent in Brazil, spirits are "summoned" through music and trance states. In shamanism, which dates back tens of thousands of years, spirit contact is facilitated through drumming, dance, meditation, the development of psychic ability and other forms of ritual.

7. You can create your own rituals, too. You might, for instance, have a designated area in your home or garden reserved for contact with the other side. The area could feature fresh flowers, statues that are personally significant, a prayer rug, or objects that belonged to the person you wish to contact. Experiment; it's an adventure.

8. The greater your sense of adventure, the more successful you'll be at spirit contact. Medium Hazel Burley, who lives in the spiritualist community of Cassadaga, Florida—which we cover in Chapter 7, on mediums— felt a calling toward mediumship. She was just a young woman when she moved to this town of spiritualists

to study with a renowned medium, Wilbur Hull, and embarked on the greatest adventure of her life.

You don't have to become a medium to make contact. However, by seeing a reputable medium at work, you might open yourself to more contact. Once you've experienced direct spirit contact, you won't ever see the world in quite the same way again.

2

VICTORIAN
AWAKENING

An extraordinary development took place in the Western world near the end of what was known as the Victorian Age. Prevalent religious, scientific, and cultural forces in the mid-nineteenth century ridiculed and dismissed any claims of personal contact with the unseen, the unknown, the realms beyond the physical world. Yet, the spirits came out of the closet. The event that triggered widespread interest in contact with the other side took place in 1848 in Hydesville, New York, a hamlet that no longer exists.

The Fox Family

It began after John and Margaret Fox and two of their three daughters moved into a cottage that was available because previous residents were disturbed by sounds they heard at night. Soon the Foxes were also plagued by a mysterious rapping.

One night, John Fox was determined to find its source. He rattled the windows, expecting to find the sashes loose. After he stopped, he heard a similar noise—a rattle—as if in reply. His twelve-year-old daughter Kate then clapped her hands. The same number of taps responded, as if rapped by invisible knuckles against a wall. The same thing happened when her older sister Maggie tried, writes Roy Stemman in *Spirits and Spirit Worlds*.

Eventually, the Fox family learned from the entity that he was a murdered peddler named Charles B. Rosna, whose body was buried beneath the cabin. Despite finding some initial evidence that a body had been buried there, it took another fifty-six years before a skeleton was found.

While mysterious rapping sounds in old houses had been detected by many others, the Fox case was unique in that they were able to communicate with the unseen rapper. News of the mysterious rappings became the talk of the small town and over the course of the next few years, interest in contact with spirits spread fast and furiously. The rapping not only disrupted the lives of the Fox family, it instigated a new metaphysical movement that became known as spiritualism. Throngs of people on both sides of the Atlantic set out to make contact with departed family members and friends, and with guiding spirits. March 31, 1848, the day communication began, is now considered the birthday of spiritualism. By 1855, 2 million people were followers of the movement.

Maggie Fox later claimed the sisters had faked the rapping, but the following year she retracted the confession. The explanation that the sisters could crack their toes to make the rapping sound didn't explain the body dug up below the house, or the intensity of the rapping. The sound was described as "loud enough to be heard several rooms off" by William Crookes, a prominent British scientist, who examined Kate Fox between 1871 and 1874, and became convinced the rapping phenomenon was not faked.

From the heyday of spiritualism to the present, skeptics have been quick to grasp onto any explanation—no matter how outlandish—that avoided the reality of spirit contact. Once a few con artists were exposed, many critics of spiritualism proclaimed all mediums were frauds—the equivalent of saying that since some doctors are quacks, all of them are.

White Crows

By the turn of the twentieth century, the heyday of spiritualism was coming to an end. Repeated attacks by ardent skeptics who exposed fraud and antispiritualism pronouncements from religious leaders who instilled fear of the devil diminished enthusiasm for contacting the spirit world.

In spite of the condemnations, some investigators remained open-minded, and searched for what they called the one "white crow"—an authentic medium.

One such investigator was philosopher William James, a founding member of the American Society for Psychical Research, a group of scientists who investigated mediums. He is known for saying, "If you wish to upset the law that all crows are black, you must not seek to show that no crows are; it is enough if you prove one single crow to be white." Eventually,

James came to believe that he found his white crow in a medium named Leonora Piper. When introduced to her, he was initially skeptical, but he was impressed that she didn't use any of the typical Victorian spiritualist paraphernalia such as spirit cabinets, bells, and trumpets. After attending additional séances, James concluded that she had the ability to communicate with the dead. While mainstream science continues to doubt the existence of any such white crows, your own experiences might confirm our belief that a 'white crow' can be found within each of us.

DETECTING SPIRITS

During the time that spiritualism was under heavy attack, one surprising supporter stepped forward. Arthur Conan Doyle, creator of Sherlock Holmes, announced he was a follower of spiritualism. The irony, of course, was that among fictional detectives, Holmes was known for his emphasis on cold facts. However, he also once said, "When you have eliminated the impossible, whatever remains, however improbable, must be true."

For Conan Doyle, communication with the dead was, however improbable, clearly not impossible. He was raised in a Catholic family, but as an adult called himself an agnostic. However, spiritualism offered him firsthand evidence and answers to his questions about the soul's survival. His support of spiritualism damaged his reputation, but he refused to back off. Shortly before his death in 1930, Conan Doyle wrote, "The reader will judge that I have had many adventures. The greatest and most glorious of all awaits me now."

While we were writing about Conan Doyle, we received an e-mail entitled "Good News," written by someone named Donna Doyle. Of course, the name caught our attention. The message was a request for books for a benefit auction. So, related events came together in a way that couldn't be explained by cause and effect. Not only were we writing a book and the e-mail writer was asking about books, she had the same last name as the author we were writing about at that time. That, for us, was a synchronicity, and a hint that we were on the right track. So, of course, we sent her *The 7 Secrets of Synchronicity*, our first book on the subject.

Jung's Spirits

Carl Jung maintained a longtime fascination with spiritualism, and the subject was central to his medical dissertation. But that paper and other early writings on the subject presented a skeptical point of view regarding spirit contact.

Deirdre Bair, author of *Jung: A Biography*, noted that Jung as a student was more enthusiastic than dismissive about spiritualism, but his dissertation "required prudence in intellectualizing the ideas about spiritualism and occult phenomena that he embraced so emotionally. . . ."

According to Bair, Jung's interest in psychiatry as a specialty dated from his first year in medical school, when two inexplicable events happened that led him to read widely about spiritualism, at the time considered an adjunct to psychiatry.

One summer afternoon, Jung was studying in his room when he heard a loud noise, like pistol shots, coming from the dining room. He ran out into the dining room, where a seventy-year-old walnut table, a family heirloom, had split down the middle for no obvious reason. The day was hot and humid, as opposed to a cold, dry, winter day when something like that would be more likely to happen.

A few weeks later, Jung got home to find his mother, sister, and the maid in turmoil. They had heard a similar noise but had been too frightened to look for the cause. At the side cupboard, Bair writes, "There lay a bread knife, its blade neatly severed in several places in a manner that could not have occurred naturally."

Jung took the knife to a cutler, who insisted the knife could only have been broken intentionally. After this, Jung began to read widely about spiritualism, and believed there was something to it.

From descriptions in Bair's biography, it seems that Jung's mother, Emilie, was probably psychic. As a youngster, she had visions, and she grew up in a large clan of nephews, nieces, and cousins who had similar visions. Jung's interest in spirit contact dated back to his years as a student when he would gather with others for Saturday night séances. He even made a Ouija board by writing the letters on cardboard and using an overturned glass as a planchette.

In spite of those influences, as Jung moved into the professional world of psychotherapy, he publicly took a skeptical point of view on contact with the other side. Only later in his career would his true beliefs become widely known.

THEORY OF CORRESPONDENCE

In the mid-eighteenth century, Emanuel Swedenborg, a Swedish scientist and philosopher, developed what he called the theory of correspondence, which laid the groundwork for the rise of spiritualism a century later.

Swedenborg proposed that a strong link exists between the physical world and the spirit world. He said that our decisions influence spirits and their desires influence our lives. In essence, he was suggesting the existence of an interdimensional "butterfly effect" in which a small change in one place can have a big effect in another place.

The End of Spiritualism?

A final note on the rampant fraud that existed during the spiritualist era. After Maggie Fox came forward before a packed crowd in 1888 and declared that she and her sisters had faked all the rapping noises, the media of the day shouted with glee. *Spiritualism Exposed. The Fox Sisters Sound the Death-Knell of the Mediums,* shouted the *New York World* in large, bold headlines on Sunday, October 21. "The severest blow that Spiritualism has ever received is delivered to-day through the solemn declaration of the greatest medium of the world that it is all a fraud, a deception and a lie," wrote the *World*.

When Maggie retracted her confession a year later, it was hard to know what to believe about the sisters. Were they true mediums or frauds right from the beginning? Or did they mix fakery with real spirit contact to keep their performances lively?

When William James began attending séances in the late 1860s, most turned out to be rife with fakery, a depressing situation for an investigator intent on finding at least one true medium. Yet, James had little regard for skeptics who summarily rejected all claims of spirit contact. Remarking on the situation, he wrote, "There is no source of deception in the investigation of nature which can compare with a fixed belief that certain kinds of phenomenon are *impossible*."

What's Your Attitude?

This exercise allows you to determine your attitude regarding spirit contact. Imagine that you meet someone who seems like a nice person. You've been talking for a few minutes when she tells you that she's been feeling sad because her favorite uncle died. But now she feels much better because she got a message from him.

What's your first reaction?

1. Watch out for this one; she's weird.
2. I want to know more. How did she get the message and what was it?
3. Not interested. Let's change the subject.
4. Time to go. End of conversation.
5. This is my kind of friend.
6. Nobody can get messages from the other side.
7. There is no afterlife, so what's she talking about?
8. God does not allow for such contact.
9. She might be talking to the devil.
10. Wait until she hears my story.
11. I wonder if she could get a message from one of my dead relatives.
12. I feel sorry for her; she's deluding herself.
13. It's possible, but there's no way to prove it.
14. I hope this is a joke.
15. I just heard someone on TV talking about the same subject. Is that a coincidence or synchronicity?

If you checked:

1, 4, or 7, you are a nonbeliever.

3, 12, or 14, you're probably not interested in the subject and someone who's reading the book showed you the above list.

6, 8, or 9, you're highly suspicious of anyone who talks to spirits.

2, 13, or 15, you're skeptical, but open-minded.

5, 10, or 11, you're a believer, but you might be gullible.

Unearthing Your Hidden Family History

You may learn about a history of contact within your family by asking older relatives about their experiences. Start out by identifying your older relatives, including ones whom you haven't seen for a long time. Whenever possible, schedule a visit. If you need to give a reason for the visit, say that you're looking into the family's history and you would like to hear stories from the past.

Once you've established your purpose, your great-uncle or elderly second cousin may recollect how his or her grandfather buried gold beneath the porch or died in a faraway war. When the topic of death comes up, ask if anyone in the family has ever seen a ghost. Was the ghost a deceased family member? Were any messages received?

Don't be surprised if you experience synchronicities or serendipity in your search. After all, loved ones and ancestors are probably cheering you on. They might have even nudged you into pursuing the matter. You might be looking in one direction, and answers come to you unexpectedly from another source. You might discover that a certain aunt, who relatives whisper about at family gatherings, has an unusual talent: She can talk to the dead. Some family members think "she's not right in the head," but others say she knows things she shouldn't.

If you know of such a relative in your family, she might hold a treasure of information, not only about your extended family but about contact with the afterlife. When you approach her, you can probably be much more open about your interests. After decades of being shunned or belittled, she will probably be pleased that someone in the family is finally interested. Let her know how much you appreciate the chance to talk about the mysteries of contact with the other side.

Arrive prepared with questions:

- Does she still hear from the other side?
- Who does she communicate with—deceased relatives, spirit guides, a friend who has passed on? All of the above?
- What kind of messages does she receive? Are they personal?
- Do the spirits talk about the other side?
- Do they predict future events?
- How does she receive the information?
- Does she hear a voice or see images? Does the information come through automatic writing? Can she see spirits?

By this time, you should be able to assess your informant's stability and reliability. Is she agitated or acting oddly? If so, it's time to thank her and take your leave.

However, if she seems emotionally and mentally stable, you might ask if she can make contact for you. If that's your intent, what are you interested in finding out? You might ask if the spirit or spirits have any hidden knowledge about the past they want to reveal. It could be about family history or the larger picture of past events. Or ask questions about your own life— romance, career, finances. Can they accurately describe your situation? If so, what's coming up for you in the next few weeks or months?

Take note of the responses. Remain open-minded, but don't take any information you receive as definitive proof. Over time, you can judge the accuracy of the spirits.

Hiding or Exposing Our Convictions

During a trip years ago to Mesa Verde National Park in southwestern Colorado, we joined a tour that climbed through the famed cliff dwellings of the Anasazis. When we came to a circular depression, the guide explained that we were looking into a *kiva*, an underground chamber where sacred rituals were performed. One older man looked down and shook his head, "It's nothing but a hole in the ground." Then he walked off. Another man nearby smiled, "One man's religion, another man's hole in the ground."

With that story in mind, take a look at your perception about contact with the spirit world and how you relate your thoughts to others who might have far different ideas about the subject.

Which of the following best describes you:

1. I keep my interest in the subject to myself. Most everyone I know would think I was crazy if they knew I read these kinds of books or that I've gone to mediums.
2. If the opportunity presents itself, I might engage people in the question of communication with the other side. Deep down I believe it, but I tend to take a skeptical point of view.
3. I'm involved in a group and we share our interests on the subject.

4. I don't believe it's possible to contact the dead. I'm only reading the book because someone gave it to me.
5. I used to talk openly to people about this kind of stuff, but after my boyfriend and some of my friends made fun of my beliefs I'm more careful about whom I talk to about the spirit world.
6. I let people know at every opportunity that life after death exists and we can make contact.

If you fit:

1 or 5, you probably would be cautious about reading this book in public.

2, you might allow others to see the cover and see how they react.

3, you'll probably bring the book to your group.

4, there's no way that you would want anyone seeing you with this book in your hand.

6, you'll probably flash the book at every opportunity and try to engage others in a conversation about spirit contact.

Spirits Versus Your Higher Self

Today, long after the Fox sisters, William James, Arthur Conan Doyle, and Carl Jung have passed into history, spiritualism is still alive, existing in the realm of nontraditional religious practices, such as Wicca or shamanism. However, you don't have to be a spiritualist to believe in spirit contact or experience it, any more than you need to be one particular religion in order to believe in God. Ironically, you don't even have to believe in spirits! Mainstream psychologists say that we are accessing a part of ourselves—our higher self—when we receive intuitive knowledge or guidance.

From our perspective, both possibilities are true. Sometimes you might access your higher self, while other times you might contact the other side.

3

ALTERED STATES

_____

If you're like most people, you're so busy in your daily life, so caught up in your own stuff, that you don't recognize possible attempts at communication from the other side. You might think, _Well, that was a weird dream,_ and go on about your business. But when we're relaxed, in an altered state, meditating or asleep and dreaming, we're more receptive to spirit contact.

For years, Jenean Gilstrap lived in a bungalow built in 1926. As soon as she moved in, she began restoring the main floor. Around this time, her daughter, Cindy, and Cindy's two small children came to live with her. One night, Jenean and Cindy were watching TV in the master bedroom and Jenean fell asleep. Suddenly, she was awakened by a bright light and saw her daughter standing in the hallway closet with the door open and the light on.

"Her back was to me and her long hair was down. She was wearing a yellow dress I'd never seen before. I was startled to see her and asked what she was looking for and where she'd gotten the dress. It had a fitted waist, a ruffle around the shoulders, and a full-length skirt with a sash tied in the back. I called her name several times, but she didn't answer. She just kept standing there."

Then Cindy spoke, and Jenean's head snapped around. She was shocked to see Cindy beside her in bed. She glanced quickly back at the closet, but the girl in the yellow dress was gone, the closet light was off, the door was shut. Had it been a dream? A vision? It felt astonishingly real to Jenean.

Several years later, Jenean started renovating the second floor of the bungalow. During a lunch break, she and her sister sat around the dining table with the crew and talked about all the junk the crew had pulled out of the attic. "Has Jenean told you the story about the girl in the long dress?" her sister asked the crew.

The foreman frowned. "Was it a long yellow dress with a big sash and shoulder ruffles? We pulled it out of the eaves in the side of the attic wall."

Whether it was a dream or not, Jenean's experience ended with a synchronicity—the girl's dress was found—which confirmed the sighting actually happened. "I never saw the girl again," Jenean said. "But I've wondered about her often."

When your mind is quiet, you're more receptive to spirit contact. During the winter of 1924, Carl Jung spent long periods alone in the tower of the home he built on the shores of Lake Zurich. He was in a deeply reflective state much of the time, and saw ghosts. "He heard music, as if an orchestra were playing; he envisioned a host of young peasant men who seemed to be encircling the tower with music, laughter, singing and roughhousing," wrote Deirdre Bair in her biography *Jung*.

Contact Through Meditation

About fifteen minutes into his meditation one night, Mike Perry heard a voice in his left ear. This had never happened to him before. Even though he didn't recognize the voice, it was utterly clear, and said, "Your dad is listening to you."

Mike's father had died more than twenty years earlier, and Mike always regretted that he wasn't there when it happened. He was still in a relaxed, meditative state, so he followed his instinct and spoke softly, telling his father how he missed him and his mother. "I thanked them for all they had done for me over the years, especially while I was growing up. I also spoke about my son and how he was doing. I then opened my eyes and that was it. I'd like to think that my dad heard what I said."

Meditation is one of the best ways to enter an altered state of consciousness. Not only are you relaxed and receptive, but you can direct your focus toward a particular objective.

During the summer of 2010, Rob taught a meditation course. Before the first class, Trish expressed her hope that she would experience a synchronicity. Midway through the meditation, she saw her mother standing in a corner of the room, laughing and waving at Trish's father, who strode briskly toward her.

Her mother had died ten years earlier of complications from Alzheimer's, and by the end of her life could no longer walk. Her hip had disintegrated and she wasn't a candidate for hip replacement surgery. Her father, who had Parkinson's, spent the last five years of his life in a wheelchair. And yet, in the meditation both of them looked robust, healthy, young, and filled with joy and life.

Once they realized Trish was aware of them, they both just faded away. The experience was important for Trish because her parents looked so happy and healthy. She had the distinct impression that they check in on her from time to time.

Once looked upon as unusual in the West, the practice of meditation has exploded in popularity. According to a January 2010 article in *Psychology Today*, more than 10 million Americans practice some form of meditation. Its health benefits are widely touted—lower blood pressure, better management of stress, increased blood flow and serotonin production, which in turn influences mood and behavior. It reduces premenstrual symptoms and enhances the immune system and the activity of cells that kill bacteria and cancer cells. And that's just for starters.

Since meditation enables you to enter a deeply relaxed state, it's easier to access your intuition and to become aware of your interconnectedness with all beings, including those no longer in the physical world. Meditation helps you develop mindfulness, a purposeful awareness of yourself, your thoughts, and your actions.

How to Meditate

Here are suggestions for beginning or enhancing a meditation practice, especially for the purpose of opening yourself to spirit contact and synchronicity:

Location
Avoid meditating in a place where you work, talk, or think a lot. Don't meditate at your desk in a home office or at the kitchen table. If you meditate while lying in bed, you may fall asleep. Sit on a comfortable chair or on a cushion on the floor.

Some people meditate on a porch or in an outside garden. Others have a room in their homes that is specifically for meditation, set up with plants, fresh flowers, and perhaps a fountain or altar. It should be an area where you won't be disturbed—no phones, no kids, no pets.

Select a Time
If you've never meditated before, if you're the antsy type, if you have doubts about the benefits, start with five minutes. Try to do it at the same time each day.

Keep a Positive Frame of Mind
The more positive and joyful you feel, the more likely it is that your meditation will achieve what you desire. Remember: like attracts like.

Clear Your Mind
This is easier said than done. As you try to enter a meditative state, **stuff** races through your head—you plan, reminisce, wonder, question, worry. You might think about what you did last night, wonder why so-and-so snapped at you, or worry

about the bills piling up on your desk. Let these types of thoughts flow through you—and away. Focus on your breathing or on a single word, such as One, God, Love, Peace, or count slowly to ten and back to one. You might even create a particular ritual that prepares you mentally and spiritually for your meditation.

State Your Intent

If you're interested in contacting someone who has passed on, have a specific person in mind, preferably someone you knew well. By the time you settle into place, you should know whom you want to contact in your meditation. If you have a photo of the person, set it down in front of you. Take a few moments to think about your relationship with this person and your present feelings about the individual. Then, release your thoughts.

Breathe

Quiet your mind and take several slow, deep breaths as you focus on your belly. Exhale fully, relaxing your belly. Inhale, holding the breath in your belly. Create warmth in your belly, expanding the area. Still holding your breath, relax into the feelings that surface. Feel the energy there. Let your body be sensitive and relaxed. Think of yourself becoming lighter and lighter. Hold your breath until it gets uncomfortable, then slowly exhale.

Focus on Your Body

Continue sitting quietly, letting the inner warmth rise from your belly in order to calm and relax your entire being. Imagine your cells, organs, tissues, and muscles relaxing. Follow this movement down your legs to your toes, up your torso to your neck and head, down your arms to your fingertips. You can even bathe your thoughts in this warm, calm, relaxing sensation.

Let Go

Concentrate lightly on your heart and focus on the image of the deceased loved one you want to reach. Let go of any feelings of guilt or sorrow you might feel regarding the person. After a few moments, release all of it. Breathe gently, be alert for images, and listen for a voice that's speaking to you.

If nothing happens or you're interrupted, realize that contact might come in another means, possibly through synchronicity—reading the person's name in the newspaper or on the Internet, hearing the name on the radio or television. Think of your everyday experiences as a dream and watch for signs and symbols that you might connect to a deceased loved one.

The next time you enter a meditative state, imagine a cord connecting you and a deceased loved one at the solar plexus. Maybe an image will come to mind or you'll hear a voice reassuring you, offering a message. Maybe nothing happens immediately, but after your session an object appears in an unusual place and you recognize it as a sign or symbol, a link to your departed loved one.

Alternately, as you move into a meditative state, picture the sky overhead where you can see a tiny rectangular object at the zenith. You can project yourself upward to this object, which is a platform. You might find the spirit of your loved one waiting for you there. The platform is your place of connection. You can visit at any time and from the platform you can leap off into other worlds, other dimensions.

Your Dream Life: Taking Inventory

Dreams provide our most immediate access to spirit communication. This idea has been accepted in cultures worldwide since ancient times. Consider your beliefs about dreams:

- Do you believe that they are mostly the mind's way of processing the day's events?
- Do you think they can be prophetic?
- Do you think they can be literal?
- Are they mostly symbolic?
- Do you believe that in a dream state you can make contact with someone who has passed on?

If you answered yes to all of those questions, you have a strong and accurate awareness of dreaming. In other words, dreams are many things. There are everyday dreams, where your mind rehashes the day's events; there are also Big Dreams, important ones that relate to the direction of your life. Those dreams, in particular, can involve spirit contact.

The Aborigines believe they receive guidance and information through dreams in which their ancestors speak to them. In Greek and Roman times, special temples were built where people could sleep and receive messages through their dreams. The ancient Chinese believed that dreams were actual places where the spirit went to receive knowledge and wisdom. Among many Native American cultures, dreams are considered separate realities. Black Elk, of the Oglala Sioux, became a respected medicine man through what his dreams revealed to him. People have long believed that dreams are a way of connecting with the spirit world.

In recent decades, the concept of dreaming as a vehicle to spirit communication has gained a wider acceptance in Western culture. In fact, if you Google the phrase "spirit contact in dreams," more than 50 million hits come up. That's roughly the population of Los Angeles, Mexico City, New York City, Moscow, Rio de Janeiro, and Mumbai.

In the dream state, we drop our inhibitions and limiting beliefs, making it a realm where communication happens. Whether we are aware of it or not, we are in nightly contact with the spirit world.

Contact in Dreams

Because there are fewer cognitive barriers, because we are less likely to disbelieve, the dream state serves as a rich medium for exploring contact with the other side. The TV show *Medium* always begins with a dream in which a spirit is communicating something to Allison Dubois. The dreams usually hold clues of some kind—names and locations, faces, the nature of a crime, the truth about how someone died. The idea is that spirits attempt to communicate with the character because she's a psychic who sees ghosts regularly in her waking life. But the bottom line is that spirits attempt to communicate with her because *she's open and receptive to contact.*

This receptivity is the most important quality you can nurture in yourself to communicate with deceased loved ones in dreams. If you're attempting to make contact in your dreams with deceased loved ones, it's important to nurture a sense of openness and receptivity. You can do so by "incubating" dreams featuring spirit contact just before you go to sleep. As you settle into bed for the night, ask for contact. Say the name or names of those you would like to hear from. Picture the person or persons in your mind. Say you would like to receive a message or messages, and that you are open and receptive. Add that you are only interested in positive and beneficial communication from loved ones—no intruders are welcome.

Here are additional suggestions for enhancing the possibility of spirit contact while you dream:

Request a Visitation Dream

Before you fall asleep, explain how you feel—that you would like verification that the person's soul continues, that you need that verification to heal. Then take the necessary steps to ensure that you remember the night's dreams. Have a flashlight, notepad, pen, even a recorder next to the bed. Fall asleep with clear intentions.

If you aren't successful in remembering your dreams at first, keep at it. Eventually, you'll train yourself to awaken after important dreams.

Several months after Trish's mother died, she asked for a visitation dream. She wanted to know if her mother's mental confusion from Alzheimer's had disappeared upon death. After a week of requesting a dream each night, she dreamed that her mother was wandering through a hallway, using a walker as she had toward the end of her life. She was distraught, calling out for her husband, Trish's dad. The atmosphere was odd, not well lit, and seemed to smell of mold. Her mother couldn't find the door or anyone to help her.

Trish felt the visitation was real, but because her mother was still so confused, she sensed that her mother hadn't been aware of her. The stink of mold seemed to represent the past, and the fact that the hallway was so dimly lit suggested that her mother couldn't find the way out and leave her confusion behind her.

The encounter wasn't what Trish had hoped to discover, so it was several months before she asked for another visitation dream.

During the second dream encounter, the atmosphere was vastly changed. Through a large window, Trish could see her mother hurrying along a line of people that snaked up the street toward a theater. Her mother seemed to be in charge of making sure everyone got inside. She was animated, walking normally.

The synchronicity in these dream visitations is that a request results in a dream experience that provides the information you're seeking. You might argue that your request prompts your subconscious to spin the dream, so cause and effect rather than synchronicity is involved. But a dream visitation usually resonates intuitively. You feel certain you have experienced contact with the dead.

Once you've made contact, be content with the reassurances you received that deceased loved ones continue to exist in a nonphysical world and that any injuries and pains they experienced in life are behind them. Offer well wishes and thanks for the message, then let it go. Don't repeatedly ask for contact with the dead. Even though you might miss a spouse, family member, or friend, you need to allow spirits to move on with their journeys.

It's fine to ask our departed loved ones for reassurance that they are well and thriving on the other side. But to do so repeatedly may interrupt their journeys in the afterlife.

Dream Visitations from Strangers

Dream visitations also occur when you don't request them and often involve people you've never met. During Jennifer Gerard's first trip to Thailand twenty years ago, she was exhausted upon her arrival and went to bed as soon as possible. Shortly after she fell asleep, she was aware of her surroundings, as if she was seeing the sparse room and the two beds through the backs of her eyelids. Everything in the room was exactly as it had been when she lay down, except that she had visitors. She realized she was experiencing a lucid dream—one in which it seems you're awake within a dream.

A monk, seemingly deceased, lay on the bed next to hers. Around him, three other monks in long, dark red robes with large yellow hats were marching clockwise around the body. One of them swung an incense burner as they walked and chanted. They were completely absorbed in what they were doing until they came around the foot of the bed. One of the monks realized Jennifer was there and looked right into her eyes with a fierce and fixed gaze. "I cannot ever remember the feeling of being seen in any other dream than this one," she told us. "Usually it is the dreamer who does all of the seeing."

In seconds, she bolted awake and ran downstairs to the lobby. She asked the teenagers at the desk how old the building was and if anyone had ever seen any ghosts there. They said that the building was quite old, but they hadn't heard about any ghosts. They also pointed out that Thai monks wear orange robes and don't have big yellow hats. She couldn't go back to sleep that night.

Several years later, Jennifer was on a buying trip in Nepal for her jewelry business in Ohio. On the wall of a different hotel was a mural of the same red-robed monks with large yellow hats she'd seen in her dream. On that trip, she was treated to dinner by a member of the Dalai Lama's family. Jennifer was so surprised by the painting that she told the relative about her dream. The woman felt sure it was a reincarnation dream and that perhaps Jennifer's son was a reincarnate. "She urged me to contact His Holiness's office. I still have his business card, but I wasn't prepared for the prospect of a special Buddhist education for my child." She never made the call.

Drug-Induced Altered States

Meditation and dreaming are not the only ways to enter an altered state. A hot shower, a massage, a long drive can do it. It happens for some people while doing yoga, cooking, gardening, watching TV, reading, relaxing by a swimming pool or on the warm sand at the beach. Lack of sleep can do it, too.

Certain types of drugs, of course, can lead to altered states. When Debra Page, a Dharma student in California, ended up in the emergency room in horrendous pain, she was given morphine. She says, "And suddenly, I was surrounded by the dead, all of them talking at once, all of them with messages for their loved ones."

We don't recommend any kind of drug to induce an altered state of consciousness. In fact, when you're trying to communicate with spirits, it's wise to stay away from any mind-altering substance, including alcohol. Spirit contact through drug use can attract unwanted entities and create distortions and nightmarish scenarios. You might also experience hallucinations unrelated to spirit contact. Find a method that puts *you* in control of the situation, so that you don't have to question whether your experience is real or imagined.

Grief as an Altered State

Perhaps one of the reasons that spirit communication often takes place after a loved one dies is that grief induces an altered state. You begin to question your beliefs, your perceptions, the very nature of your reality. The shadow you glimpse in your peripheral vision, the noise you hear in the hallway in the stillness of the night, the heavy breathing you feel against your cheek: it could all be just your imagination. Or not.

In 2009, Judy, a photographer, lost her close friend and fellow photographer, Hank. Their relationship—as friends, lovers, partners—had endured for thirty-five years. Without him in her life, she felt adrift. A few nights after he died, she experienced the first of several "blinking light" episodes.

"My sister had given Hank a lamp filled with seashells that reminded me of the summers Hank and I used to spend on Martha's Vineyard. I always turn the light off before I go to bed, then fall asleep with the TV on. Sometime around midnight, the light came on and woke me." This had never happened before. Judy felt certain it was Hank.

The second incident occurred shortly after she had cleaned out Hank's place. Judy was making a time capsule from some of Hank's belongings, and decided to include a button that read "Hank's Soda," a beverage he loved. "When I put it into the briefcase I was using for the time capsule, the button started to blink. I didn't even know there was a light inside it. The button continued to blink until I closed the briefcase two days later to send to a friend who lives where his ashes were to be buried."

By her own admission, Judy needed confirmation that Hank survived—and got it, through the synchronicity of blinking lights, a perfect metaphor for Hank's profession. Such synchronicities give you strength to carry on, and confidence that life continues. You gain the knowledge that loved ones are healed, and in recognizing as much, you are healed of wounds inflicted by the death of someone close to you.

It's as if death changes certain fundamental principles about the nature of reality, and creates a fertile environment for both synchronicity and contact.

Visions

Scientific speculation has accompanied a mysterious phenomenon, known as the Third Man Syndrome, in which a shadowy presence, an angel or "spirit guide," offers help and encouragement during stressful, life-or-death situations.

After flying solo for 22 hours over the Atlantic, Charles Lindbergh was fighting fatigue and inclement weather that forced him to fly so low he could feel spray from the white caps. That was when his plane "filled with ghostly presences— vaguely outlined forms, transparent, moving" that advised him on his flight, discussed navigational problems, and reassured him. Years later, Lindberg wrote, "I've never believed in apparitions, but how can I explain the forms I carried with me through so many hours of this day?"

Visions of ghosts and spirits are nothing new. Throughout history, man has had visions of the deceased. These spirits can be friendly and helpful or mischievous, even frightening. Sometimes the spirits seem to be aware of us, but just as often they aren't. They seem to be going about their business, in their own reality, oblivious to what's going on around them. That's certainly how it looked to Carrie Cousins during the last three days of her mother's life. "My aunt and I were sitting in the room when there was a loud crack in the air over my mother's head. We both looked up from our books—and saw a man leaning over my mother's bed. He wore the white and red robes of a Catholic cardinal or bishop and was giving my mother rites of some kind. As a medium, I was accustomed to seeing spirits, but I wasn't used to being with other people who could see them."

Carrie's aunt, a Baptist, saw the man as clearly as Carrie did. She burst into tears and flew out of the room. The man appeared every day at exactly the same time and gave Carrie's mother last rites. He was there at the moment she died. "His energy was so powerful that several medical personnel saw him and pretty soon, word got around and people came from all over the hospital to catch a glimpse of him."

Near-Death Experiences

Probably the most dramatic altered state of conscious—short of the ultimate journey—is a near-death experience. Raymond Moody investigated more than a hundred cases of people who had been declared clinically dead and were subsequently revived. Thanks to his book, *Life After Life*, published in 1975, the phrase "near-death experience"—or NDE—entered public consciousness. A pattern emerged from Moody's work that other physicians and researchers have built on.

According to the International Association for Near-Death Studies, a typical near-death experience involves "perceptions of movement through space, of light and darkness, a landscape, presences, intense emotion, and a conviction of having a new understanding of the nature of the universe." Many NDEs begin with an out-of-body experience in which the individual hovers nearby, watching whatever is going on around his or her body. The individual may encounter beings—spirits of deceased family members, friends, or other loved ones who have passed on, or even unknown spirits.

In 1966, JoAnne, who lives in Tennessee, gave birth to her first baby, a son. She carried him for ten months before her "quack OB" decided to induce labor. The baby was fine, but large. Three days after he was born, she began to bleed out. "As the code team frantically tried to give me more blood and shoot epinephrine directly into my heart, blood came out of me faster than they could get it in. My body was dead. My heart ceased to beat. I flatlined. I don't recall how I moved out of my body, but I vividly recall hovering near the ceiling and watching the doctors and nurses in their panic."

Yet, she felt no awareness of her physical distress. She said it was "pure bliss." She finally stopped looking at what was happening below her and felt herself gliding farther and farther away from the room. She didn't pass through a tunnel, as others have described in their NDEs. "It was more as if I stepped through a door or a gate onto a kind of brightly lit path or beam that seemed to be tugging me towards the most brilliant spectrum of colors, indescribable. I was so eager to reach those colors. But a voice, coming from someone I didn't see, very clearly said to me, 'JoAnne, you can't stay here. You have a new little boy to raise, and two more little boys coming. You have to go back.'"

But JoAnne had no desire to go back. She was infused with such comfort, peace, and joy that she felt angry at being pulled back. She looked down and was in the room again, then very suddenly, with a severe jolt that seemed like an electrical shock, she was back in her ravaged body.

She later learned that she had been clinically dead for six minutes: "There are no words in any language that can adequately describe the experience of being dead," she says.

What's especially interesting about her NDE is that the voice urging her to go back was right. She went on to have two more boys. All three of her children are now adults. JoAnne spent years working as a hospice nurse. You can't convince her that what she experienced was a blip in her synapses or some hallucinogenic tale her brain spun as it was deprived of oxygen.

Even Carl Jung, who had an NDE in 1944, said: "I can describe the experience only as the ecstasy of a non-temporal state in which past, present, and future are one. Everything that happened in time had been brought together into a concrete whole. Nothing was distributed over time, nothing could be measured by temporal concepts."

Vicki DeLaurentis drowned at the age of sixteen. She recalls drifting upward and seeing herself lying on the beach as CPR was administered. A wonderful feeling of peace and warmth spread through her. Someone behind her kept asking her different questions, then the voice told her to look more closely at the girl on the beach. "I slowly realized she looked like me—and then BAM! I was on the beach looking up at the sky." Water rushed out of her nose, ears, and eyes. The paramedics clamped an oxygen mask on her. "One reason why I personally feel it was real and not a hallucination is that I still remember it like it just happened—that was thirty-six years ago."

Death, of course, is the ultimate altered state, but a near-death experience comes close. Many who have found themselves on the edge of the other side express deep disappointment when they return. They often say that they thought they were going home—their *real* home—only to discover that they had more work to do in their physical existence. To that end, we might think of our reality in this truism from ancient yoga philosophy: Rather than physical beings seeking a spiritual experience, we are spiritual beings experiencing a physical existence. Another way of putting it: Man has no soul, but the soul has man.

Whether it's through meditation, your dreams, or other methods, altered states of consciousness provide a springboard for spirit contact. The key factor is stating your sincere interest in making contact at the outset of your meditation or before going to sleep. When that contact is made, the message will come to you as words or images or through signs or symbols.

4

HEALING SPIRITS

Modern medicine with its high-tech wonders is capable of detecting, monitoring, and curing numerous medical disorders. It does so largely by attacking the symptoms. Conventional doctors aren't known for talking about the spiritual causes of illness or for treatment and cures connected to spirit realms. That's the domain of shamans, mystics, and holistic healers. Sometimes those in need seek out such healers, hoping for improvement in their physical conditions. Other times, healing occurs spontaneously, and without the knowledge of those involved. That's how it began for José Arigo, who became one of the most renowned and documented psychic healers.

Psychic Healers

José Arigo, born in 1918 in Minas Gerais, Brazil, to a family of poor farmers, left school after third grade. At fourteen, he began working at a mine, where he labored for several years. Without a doubt, he seemed a most unlikely individual to become a world-famous healer.

When he was thirty, he began to suffer from intense headaches, insomnia, nightmares, sleepwalking, and hallucinations. He went to a doctor, but when the problems continued, he visited a local spiritist named Olivera. She prayed for him and told him that the cause of the problem was a spirit attempting to work through him.

In fact, Arigo was also hearing a voice in his head. One day he not only heard a voice, but he had a vision of a bald man, dressed in a white apron, supervising a team of doctors and nurses in an enormous operating room. This entity identified himself as Dr. Adolf Fritz, a German physician who had died in 1918, the year Arigo was born. After that incident, Arigo began to perform operations using scalpels and needles, and his headaches and other symptoms disappeared. His operations were swift, some lasting only a minute. His reputation soared and spread throughout Brazil after it was alleged that he had removed a cancerous tumor from the lung of a well-known Brazilian senator.

To perform his surgeries, Arigo opened a small clinic in his home town of Congonhas do Campo. He carried out his swift operations free of charge. He possessed no medical knowledge whatsoever, worked in unsanitary conditions, and used only his hands, a rusty knife, or occasionally a pair of scissors; his only concession to cleanliness was to wipe his knife on his shirt before and after surgery. Despite these apparently dangerous conditions, he performed hundreds of thousands of successful operations over a twenty-year period, regularly treating hundreds of people a day. During the operations, there was little bleeding and the patients didn't feel any pain. There was no need for stitches and wounds healed remarkably fast; there is also no record of a patient ever contracting an infection, despite the unsterile conditions.

The Arigo story is not only sensational, but well documented. Of course, be cautious in dealing with anyone claiming to be a psychic healer. While there are authentic healers, working in coordination with spirit guides, there are also frauds and charlatans ready to take advantage of people desperate for help.

Even though you might not want to spend your life as a psychic healer, you can reach out to spirit guides for personal healing. Some people consider these guides as part of their inner selves or higher selves, while others see them as separate beings. Could it be possible that they are both?

Doctors Without Bodies

Before we go any further, take a moment to check your thoughts about healing through spirits. Which fits you best:

- ❑ I've heard that psychic healers are all frauds, and that's probably true. I would never go to one.
- ❑ I'm sure there are some genuine psychic healers, but I doubt that spirits have anything to do with their work. If I was convinced a healer was the real deal, I might try one.

❏ I'm a believer. I've heard true stories about psychic healings through spirit guides. I wouldn't hesitate to go to a psychic healer.

❏ I don't know if they're real or not, but just the thought of going to one of them for a healing, especially surgery, freaks me out. No thank you!

❏ If I were ill and had run out of options with traditional medicine, I would go to a psychic healer.

You don't necessarily need to be seriously ill to visit a psychic healer. Consultations can also address your psychological health as well as any physical ailments. A psychic healer might simply introduce you to your spiritual guides. Whether you take such a step obviously depends on your attitudes and beliefs.

If the thought of visiting a psychic healer makes you fearful, you're probably not ready for the experience. You need to examine the nature of your beliefs. Maybe you've been influenced by skeptical views suggesting that all psychic healers are frauds who use tricks and sleight of hand and are after your money. On the other extreme, maybe your religious upbringing has led you to believe that psychic healers are in league with diabolical forces. Through our experiences, we've come to believe that healing powers exist within each of us, no matter what our beliefs or religious background, and that some people have abilities to trigger healing through their contact with spirit beings.

Embarking on a healing journey can attract synchronicities that allow you to find your path toward health and wellness. Synchronicity might lead you to the right healer or to the right therapy. It might even signal a significant shift in your consciousness that allows your healing to occur without intervention from either a physician or a nontraditional healer.

OH MY PAPA

One day, Liz visited a friend, a Reiki healer and a medium. While on the table, Liz silently asked her father to be with her, if he possibly could. She didn't mention this to her friend.

A few moments into the healing, her friend began to describe the presence of a healing spirit, a young-looking man with warm brown eyes and thick, dark auburn hair, who was wearing a Masonic ring on the ring finger of his right hand. She added that he was wearing khakis and western boots.

"My dad died at age forty-two," says Liz. "He was a 33rd-degree Mason and wore his ring on his right hand. He had brown eyes and auburn hair, and was a cattleman who went to work in khakis and western boots. I knew he was with us."

When it was over, Liz got in her car to drive home and turned on the radio. It was silent for a second, then the old song by Eddie Fisher, *Oh My Papa*, came on and filled the car with those beautiful, comforting words. "I sat there and laughed and cried, knowing my dad was right there. That was no coincidence."

It was synchronicity.

The Body Speaks: Intuition, Spirit, and Synchronicity

Any evening on television, you're besieged by commercials about pharmaceuticals that treat a wide range of illnesses and diseases. Restless leg syndrome. Obesity. Diabetes. Insomnia. Menopause. Never mind that some of these conditions, like menopause, are simply physical cycles, not illnesses. Not a single one of these commercials ever addresses the emotional or spiritual triggers for illness. The drug companies hope you'll pop a pill for whatever ails you.

But individuals who have been cured of serious illnesses through nontraditional methods often talk about how their higher selves—their souls or spirits—spoke to them through their bodies.

In 1975, W. Brugh Joy had a flourishing medical practice in Los Angeles; life was good. Then shortly before his thirty-fifth birthday, he was diagnosed with chronic relapsing pancreatitis, and there was no cure. This disease causes debilitating abdominal pain that may persist for several days, as it did for Joy. He knew the disease was unpredictable, that it might end abruptly on its own, or that an attack could turn into fulminating pancreatitis, which at that time had a mortality rate of 80 percent. With each attack, Joy probed his own psyche, struggling to understand why he was manifesting a disease that could severely restrict his activities or lead to his demise.

"I examined the stresses in my life, but they were inconsequential in comparison to the disease process and thus not powerful enough to lead to it. I talked to my body, trying to find some symbolic aspect that a malfunctioning pancreas might reflect, but nothing appeared. I simply could not see the dynamics of my problem," he says.

One Saturday morning while working on some medical charts in his office, he felt a powerful urge to enter into meditation. Even though he meditated daily, this urge was exceptionally strong, so he finished up what he was doing and began meditating. "A vortex of energy, of a magnitude I had never before experienced, reverberated through my body and threw my awareness into a super heightened state. Then a loud voice said, in essence, 'Your experience and training as an orthodox physician is completed. It's over. The time has come for you to embark on a rededication of your Beingness to a deeper commitment and action.'"

The voice proceeded to lay out the journeys Joy would be taking—Findhorn, UK; Egypt; India; Nepal—trips that would "reawaken old soul memories." The voice told him that his vision of being a physician was distorted and overemphasized "the body and external causes and ignored the journey of the soul." He was to start studying alternative healing techniques and practices so that he could develop a more integrated approach to healing.

The experience was so powerful that within six weeks, Joy had resigned from his medical practice and walked away from all that was familiar to him. "The wellspring that nourished my awareness was the knowing—the absolute *knowing*—that the course of action I was following was true to my soul." When he arrived in Findhorn, his first destination, he realized he hadn't had a single attack of abdominal pain since that voice first spoke to him.

His body had spoken and its message was clear: It was time to restore his soul.

Not every illness or disease, of course, results in a complete change in lifestyle or spiritual beliefs. But every illness, even the common cold, is an opportunity to decipher your body's code, to break down its messages to find out what the deeper meaning is, what your soul is trying to tell you. With a serious illness, figuring out the message is essential.

There's no one particular way to heal yourself or others. It all depends on circumstances, as Morgana Starr reveals in her personal story of how she overcame a debilitating case of fibromyalgia. "At times pain can follow every step you take. One doctor told me that I had lived with pain so long that I thought it was normal. I had pursued many natural and spiritual healing methods. Some helped; some did little to lessen the chronic pain."

Fibromyalgia was controlling Morgana's life. Dancing was out of the question. Yet, a sacred healing dance around a fire changed her life at a time when the pain was at an all-time high. "I stood outside the circle watching the dancers weave through each other. I was unable to dance, barely able to move. Every muscle and joint screamed in pain. I called out from deep within my spirit to be released from the agony."
A gentle feeling washed over her, bringing tears that began to flow down her face. Being a healer, she was used to helping others. However, because of the fibromyalgia she'd been feeling drained of any ability to assist anyone. But now, something was happening to her.

"One sweet lady came up to me, held my face, and sang to the beat of the drum. Take what you need; give what you can. Your tears are your gift for Mother Earth. Take from spirit what you need to heal."

As she danced off, Morgana took her words to heart. She slowly made her way into the circle of dancers. "I took a deep breath, and in came the energy of the angel Anael. I felt her energy tingle through every part of my body."

In front of her, she saw three female spirit guides. One carried fiery energy directed at setting boundaries for herself, one was gently enfolding her in love, and the third exuded a warrior energy. "They joined hands with each other and with me. We danced, slow and gracefully. I felt their energy surge through me, chasing out pain and weariness. Anael breathed each breath with me and I felt her heartbeat as one with mine. I was lost in a world of beauty and unconditional love."

When it was over, two women approached her and one said, "Your dancing was so beautiful! It seemed as if you were dancing with someone."

Morgana was surprised because she'd lost awareness of everyone, except for Anael and the three spirit guides. "I smiled and shared with them my healing experience in the hopes that they, too, could learn to dance with the angels and their guides and shift their lives." She was free of pain and filled with a peace that she had never experienced.

That was more than two years ago. She remains free of the intense pain and continues to work with Anael and her guides. "When I let go of their help, I find the pain returning. But as soon as I reconnect, I'm free of pain again."

Morgana's final comment echoes the words of Mona Lisa Schultz, author of *Awakening Intuition*: "If you don't learn the lesson your intuition teaches you through an illness the first time, it will return and hit you with an even bigger hammer." Some of our beliefs and the fixed ideas that define our personal realities limit our growth and evolution as human beings. Such limiting beliefs can manifest into physical symptoms, requiring us to look deeply into ourselves in order to seek balance and harmony.

Your communication with the spirit within you is more vital to your well-being than communicating with the spirit of a deceased person. But in some instances, spirit intervention can help resolve physical problems, particularly if your beliefs allow such a thing.

While brushing her teeth, Cathy accidentally knocked one of her front lower teeth with the brush and loosened it. The tooth was painful for several days and moved every time she ate or spoke. Finally, one night while lying in bed in excruciating pain, Cathy decided to call on a dentist in spirit for help.

"My husband's partner in his dental lab was a dentist, Dr. S. He was 'family' for twenty-five years, a wonderfully gifted healing physician. That night I called on Dr. S, and asked if he could please come and help me. I dreamed about him, and in the dream he was pulling that tooth. About 3:00 A.M., I woke up and noticed the tooth wasn't hurting. I put my finger in my mouth and didn't feel the tooth. I discovered it had been pulled and was lying at the front of my mouth."

Cathy said there was no pain whatsoever. She took the tooth out, set it on the bedside table, then got up to check for bleeding. She was shocked to discover the entire tooth, root and all, had been removed. There wasn't a single drop of blood. She didn't have any doubt that Dr. S had actually pulled that tooth and then had awakened her so she wouldn't swallow it.

She noted that front teeth have very deeply embedded roots and are difficult to extract. "But Dr. S has enormous energy. Grateful doesn't even begin to express my feelings. What a gift of healing from a loving spirit."

Your Body, Your Spirit

The next time you're feeling out of sorts, find a quiet place where you won't be disturbed and get into a relaxed state of mind. You're going to enter into a dialogue with your body to find out what's really going on. To do this, you can imagine your own soul or spirit as a beacon of healing light that enters that area of your body that's feeling pain. Or, you can call upon the spirit of a deceased loved one to guide you in this dialogue with your own body. Or, speak to your body directly. Do whatever feels most comfortable for you. Be intuitively open to receiving information.

Let's say you've been experiencing lower back pain. Focus on that area—rather than on the pain itself—and ask what the pain is really about. The answer may come to you in images, symbols, signs, or even as a powerful voice, like what Joy heard.

A friend of ours who employed this technique was surprised when he received an image of his workplace and his boss. He loved his work and he and his boss got along fine, so this didn't seem to explain anything. But as he continued to request information, another image surfaced, of a coworker who had been laid off a few weeks earlier. He immediately knew the back pain was related to his fear that he might be next on the chopping block.

Once our friend identified the cause, he rectified his thinking. After all, he hadn't lost his job and had no reason to believe that he might. When he banished his fear, his lower back problem began to clear up.

The lesson here is to look for deeper meaning related to physical ailments. Sometimes, when that meaning is found through synchronicity, dreams, signs, or symbols, your inner self—the spirit within—provides the healing that is necessary, and you come back into balance.

The Making of a Healer

If you feel that a medical intuitive or alternative healer may be able to help you help yourself, then allow synchronicity to be your guide to the right individual. And if you can find a healer who, like Jane Clifford, was led to healing through synchronicity, so much the better!

Jane Clifford owned an antique shop in Wales and did clairvoyant readings for many years. However, being empathic, she found it difficult to deal with the bad news that came up in her readings. "Knowing a friend or loved one was going to die is particularly distressing. So I stopped doing readings. However, premonitions continued to come."

She had used homeopathic remedies for years for curing common ailments. So when she visited Australia a few years ago, she knew she would connect with aboriginal medicine. With no plans in advance to meet any healers, one synchronicity after another led her to meet a man who gave her forty-five natural aboriginal remedies. The man not only made the remedies, he exported them to the United Kingdom.

Jane closed her antique business, stopped doing readings, and waited for the next synchronicity that would point the way for her. "For a couple of years, I had no clue. I would repeatedly say, 'How may I serve?'"

One day Jane was talking to a young woman at a party when she glimpsed an image of her hand touching a particular vertebrae on the woman's back. She didn't say anything to the woman, a stranger. But the woman abruptly changed the conversation and told Jane she'd been suffering from constant back pains for two years. But in the time they'd been talking, she said, the pain had completely disappeared.

Jane blurted that she hadn't cured her, only given her temporary relief, but the woman was astonished and happy to be pain free. Jane was also amazed. Even though she wasn't yet promoting herself as a healer, one healing led to another, as people she met mentioned their physical ailments and complaints. These random healings occurred mostly at social gatherings where she healed strangers.

So, in a sense, healing found Jane. She believes that all healing comes from higher dimensions, cosmic energy, All That Is, what she refers to as Source Energy. "And my method seems to be direct transmission. I can't take the credit for the healings; it comes through me and facilitates the patient to heal themselves, but they have to be ready."

Some people have the healing touch from childhood. For others, such as Jane, it comes later in life. You can experiment with your own abilities to heal yourself and others. With practice, you may find that you, too, have the touch.

Healing Begins at Home

Whether you have a chronic illness or are the type of person who gets one cold a year, try to uncover the emotional cause before you run off to a doctor for a quick fix. Here are some simple questions to ask yourself:

- Are you, like Joy, ignoring your spiritual life?
- Do you place blame on others whenever you're sick?
- What purpose does your illness serve? Does it prevent you from doing something you really *don't* want to do? Does it give you a chance to rest? Does it perhaps bring attention from a partner or friend who you feel is ignoring the relationship?
- Do you feel the energy/environment in your home or workplace is toxic? If so, why? Is it due to personality conflicts? Some people are like psychic sponges; they absorb the feelings and concerns of others even when those concerns aren't vocalized. If you're that type, you might want to read the section in Chapter 6 called Psychic Protection.
- Did you recently lose someone close to you? If so, then your illness could be the result of what shaman refer to as soul loss, when part of the soul is driven from the body through

unbearable sadness or grief. Be sure to read the section in Chapter 12 called Shamanic Journey.

The next time you're feeling under the weather, take a few minutes to listen to *your* body. Ask the spirit of a deceased love one to help you heal, and look for synchronicities that offer answers.

A Healing Friendship

Sometimes, spirits help in unexpected ways to heal not only our bodies, but also our lives.

They intervene in mysterious ways that may not be obvious to us until months or years later.

When Jeff was six years old, he met Jill, who climbed into his tree house and introduced herself. From then on, they were best friends. He was there when she learned to ride her bike, when her father died, when she left for college, when she graduated, when her mother died, and on the day she got married. He was there the day that Jill's daughter, Katie, was born, and there on the day that Jill's husband passed away. He was also there on the day that Jill was diagnosed with breast cancer and there on the day that Jill knew the cancer would beat her. He was there for Jill the day she asked him to take care of Katie and there on the day that Jill died.

In the winter of 2007, Jeff's wife, Jenny, was pregnant. She was in the second trimester of what had been a difficult pregnancy. It was the snowiest winter on record and the weather forecasters were calling for "the blizzard of the century," with a total of 30 inches of snow expected. "The howling wind was blowing the snow around so hard I couldn't even make out the tree line at the far end of our backyard," says Jeff. He figured it was a great day to stay home and read by the fire. Then he heard Jenny calling him from upstairs. He could tell by the sound of her voice that something was terribly wrong.

He ran up the stairs and found her sitting on the bathroom floor with blood running down her legs. Fearing the worst, he grabbed his keys and prepared for an emergency trip to the hospital in the midst of the blizzard.

"I knew there was no way an ambulance would make it up the mountain, so we were on our own. I loaded Jenny and the girls into the Jeep, and off we went. We made it to the hospital in record time, over winding, unplowed mountain roads."

He soon found out that Jenny had a placental abruption, which meant the placenta had torn and partially detached from her uterus. The baby was okay for the moment, but the damage to the cord and placenta meant she was still in great danger. Jenny was barely five-and-a-half months pregnant, so it was way too early to deliver. Jenny was kept at the hospital on complete bed rest and would have to stay there until the baby was born. They hoped and prayed for their baby to remain in utero as long as she could. Every day counted.

Four days later, Jeff was sitting by Jenny's bedside when her eyes suddenly rolled back in her head and she lost consciousness. Machines started beeping wildly, alarms shrilled, doctors and nurses rushed into the room with carts full of strange-looking equipment. Jeff was told the baby would have to be delivered immediately.

He protested that it was too soon, but the doctor said that the uterine tear had progressed, and if they didn't get the baby out now, both Jenny and the baby would die. After the baby was removed, the doctors couldn't stop the bleeding and they had to do an emergency hysterectomy. "They saved Jenny's life, and I will forever be grateful to those surgeons for that. That was the most terrifying hour of my life. The thought of losing her almost killed me."

The baby was three-and-a-half months premature. Jeff didn't even get a chance to see his daughter before they put her on a cart and whisked her away to the neonatal intensive care unit. Jenny was still in danger, so he stayed with her. If ever there was a time when Jeff wished he could be in two places at once, it was then. After what seemed like forever, the NICU doctor came into the room and Jeff could see in his eyes that the news wasn't good.

The doctor told Jeff and Jenny that the baby would die within hours. Her lungs were too underdeveloped. There was no way for her to get enough oxygen to survive outside the womb. It was only a matter of time.

"We were heartbroken. After six years of waiting and hoping and praying for another baby and coming this far along through a difficult pregnancy, we just couldn't believe we were going to have to say goodbye to her now. It was the most horrible moment of our lives."

They were asked what the baby's name was—for the birth certificate and for the death certificate. But Jeff and Jenny hadn't decided on a name yet. "It felt so strange giving the baby a name, knowing that she was going to die so soon. We had to think about it for a while before we settled on Christina."

They sat with Christina, watching the respirator breathe for her, the heart monitor record her weak and often unsteady heartbeats, watching the blood oxygen monitor register values way too low to keep her alive. She was so tiny she would have fit in the palm of Jeff's hand. Jeff and Jenny held each other while they waited and watched, prayed and cried. "I can't even begin to describe what it feels like to sit there waiting for your baby to die. There are no words."

But Christina's heart just kept beating. Her blood oxygen level remained low, but steady. The nurse said she couldn't believe Christina had made it through the night. At one point, she called the doctor in to see what he thought. They talked for a few minutes and then brought in another doctor to consult. "I remember hearing them talking, and thinking how strange it was that their job was supposed to be to keep people alive, and yet they were standing there discussing why she wasn't dead yet. It was surreal. Part of me wanted to punch them. Another part of me wanted to thank them for giving us just a little more time with her."

For weeks, Christina just kept getting stronger. Medical experts who examined her couldn't understand why she was still alive. One day, a neonatal pulmonologist who was visiting from Boston asked Jeff and Jenny if they believed in miracles. He had seen her chart and he had no other explanation. "He said it was almost as if she was getting oxygen through some kind of invisible umbilical cord that none of us could see." Four months passed, and finally, Christina was ready to come home.

On January 18, 2011, Christina celebrated her third birthday.

"One of the best pulmonologists in the world had no explanation other than to call it a miracle. Something allowed her to be conceived when doctor after doctor said it was impossible. Something allowed her to survive in a damaged womb that provided her with less than half of the oxygen and nutrients required for her to survive. Something allowed her to survive those first hours and days and weeks in the NICU, when the doctors said it was impossible."

In September 2010, Jeff and Jenny were looking through old photo albums with their daughters. Christina was pointing out pictures of people she recognized. They came across an old picture of Jill, who was in her early twenties at the time. Jill was wearing an old pair of jeans and a T-shirt; her hair was long. Jeff said it was the version of Jill he sees in his memories—the clothing, hair, facial expression all perfectly captured the essence of who she was.

Even though Christina had seen other pictures of Jill that were around the house, she didn't recognize this younger version of Jill. Christina's eyes fixed on this picture, then she said, "That's the lady from the hospital, the one that held my hand and told me to keep breathing. She comes into my room sometimes and tells me stories before I go to sleep."

Stunned, Jeff and Jenny pressed her for more details, but she refused to say more. Jeff remains convinced that Jill, from the other side, saved Christina's life. "From the very beginning, I've always believed there is some kind of connection between Jill and Christina. Her birth was a miracle, her survival was a miracle, and I've always felt as though Jill had a hand in that, somehow. Part of me says that's preposterous. But my heart so wants it to be true."

Synchronicity awakens you to the miraculous. When it's combined with spirit contact and healing, you know that you have glimpsed the realm of the divine.

5

ULTIMATE
JOURNEY

Synchronicities and spirit communication often proliferate when we're going through major transitions in our lives: a change in job, career, or financial status; a move; a marriage or divorce; a birth—or a death, the ultimate transition and journey. The death of a family member, friend, relative, even of a beloved pet brings about synchronicities and spirit contact days or even weeks before or after the death and even at the moment of death, during the soul's transition.

The death of a loved one may be the beginning of a journey into synchronicity and spirit contact that awakens you to the subtle energies that are everywhere around you. Once this door opens and you walk through it, you won't ever look at life and death in quite the same way again. Many aspects of your beliefs will change and will do so regardless of how many people around you are saying "it's just a coincidence" or "that's impossible" or "death is the end, nothing survives." You're better off trusting your own feelings and instincts about what you're experiencing. In fact, if your journey continues, the people who say these things may eventually fall away from your life. You simply won't have much in common with them anymore and will welcome new friendships and relationships with people of like mind.

Synchronicity, Death, and Dying

In terms of synchronicity, death, and communication with the other side, meaningful coincidences are most likely to occur during three distinct phases: near death, at the moment of death, and shortly after death.

When a loved one—human or animal—is approaching death, synchronicities are often warnings intended to prepare you. They may be more difficult to interpret if the person or pet isn't ill. The synchronicities can involve virtually anything. You'll recognize the power of the event, whatever it is, but you may have to interpret it as though it was a dream. Here are some common examples of these types of experiences:

CHAPTER 5: ULTIMATE JOURNEY

- A book about life after death falls at your feet as you're browsing in a bookstore. You come home to find an e-mail saying that a close friend has passed away.
- You're cleaning out your closet, attic, or garage and find a toy that one of your grandparents gave you when you were small. It has broken in half. A short time later, you hear that your grandfather has died.
- A framed photograph of your parents is accidently knocked over and the glass splits right down the middle. Not long afterward, one of your parents passes on.
- A bird flies into your window and breaks its neck. Several days later, someone you know is killed in a car accident from a broken neck.
- A flock of butterflies, creatures associated with transformation, hovers outside your window and returns every day for several days, at around the same time. At about that time, several days or weeks later, a friend dies.
- An owl, long viewed as a messenger between the living and the dead, perches in the eaves of your home for several days in a row. On the day he doesn't appear, a loved one passes on.
- Something you associate with a pet is damaged or ruined and not long afterward, the pet dies unexpectedly.

Let's take the first example and expand it a little. Suppose that when the book on life after death falls at your feet, it opens to a certain page. You're curious, pick up the book, and read a couple of paragraphs. It concerns a young man's search for the truth about life after death in the wake of his brother's murder. So how would you interpret this experience? Think of it as a dream.

Look first at the obvious symbols: a book; the fall from the shelf to the floor, right at your feet; life after death; murder. One possible interpretation might be that someone close to you will die suddenly, possibly in a violent manner, and it will launch your search into the truth about the afterlife. However, because we live in a universe where free will operates, this event could simply be hinting at a probability, and other factors come into play. Perhaps the person escapes death without being consciously aware of how close he or she came to it.

YOUR SYNCHRONICITY JOURNAL

Get into the habit of keeping a synchronicity notebook. Learn the lexicon of your own unconscious and understand that what exists in your unconscious manifests itself in your external reality.

In your journal, describe the synchronicity in detail: date, time, the weather, what you were thinking about, where you were, what you were doing, what happened. What were you feeling at the time?

Note the symbols that occurred. Maybe you were thinking of your deceased grandfather and his favorite song suddenly came on the radio. That's a synchronicity and, possibly, spirit communication. Now look a little deeper. What are the words to this particular song? If there aren't words, does the music evoke a particular memory of your grandfather?

It's probably a good idea to keep your synchronicity journal separate from a dream journal, unless the synchronicity occurs in a dream. Then record the experience in both journals. If this seems like too much trouble, then use the same journal for both, but be sure to label correctly! Check back with your journal at least once a week.

Sometimes, an event screams "Pay attention, this is important!" It's as if the universe is addressing you through signs and symbols. The more unusual the event, the more closely you should look at it and consider its meaning. A coincidence is something that you shrug off. A synchronicity is a coincidence with a message, one that alerts you to a situation, raises your awareness, possibly of something momentous.

The next time some seemingly random event occurs—like a book falling off a shelf at your feet—don't dismiss it as meaningless. If you follow through by picking up the book and paging through it, you could be taking your first step into a magnificent adventure!

Signs and Symbols in Your Life

Think of a time when your own life was in transition—not necessarily because of a death, but due to circumstances like a move, marriage, or divorce—any major event. What signs and symbols did you notice? What kinds of meaningful coincidences occurred? Jot down whatever you can remember.

If you keep a dream journal, look through it to see if any of the signs and symbols you recall from your recent dreams are repeated in your waking life (see the sidebar on "Your Synchronicity Journal" for more information on how to record these experiences). Quite often, there are repetitions. Those symbols are especially meaningful and may surface when a death is approaching. They may appear in your dreams as well as your waking life as synchronicities.

Major transitions are important symbolically precisely because they mark a shift from one way of being and living to another. They often mirror other events in our lives. While we were working on this book, for instance, Trish and Megan, our daughter, dropped by the Apple store one day to look at the new MacBooks.

While Megan was cruising around the store, trying out the various products, Trish asked the well-informed man who had been helping them how the iPad compared to a notebook computer for writing. Could it be a substitute for her notebook while traveling? Could it be used for writing books? He asked what kinds of books she wrote, so she mentioned this synchronicity book.

"What's synchronicity?" he asked.

"Meaningful coincidence."

His eyes widened. "Oh, my life is filled with those. You want to hear a couple?"

"You bet. May I use them in our book? And on our blog?"

"Sure." And Joe proceeded to share his story.

On September 1st, years ago, his mother, who had cancer, slipped into a coma. Joe flew to New York to be with her and stayed with his brother and sisters at her bedside for about a week. Her doctors didn't have any idea whether she would regain consciousness or simply pass on, and he had to return to work. He and his siblings believed their mother would die on September 19th, the day of her anniversary. So Joe flew home. "Sure enough, at 6:00 A.M. on September 19th, I got a call that mom had just passed away. What are the odds?"

Trish wasn't just impressed by the odds, but by the fact that she and Megan had stopped in the store on a whim and this employee *just happened* to be the one who had approached them first and *just happened* to have this wonderful story about spirit communication. It seems that the spirit of Joe's mother had somehow communicated to her children when she was going to pass away. In a sense, she was telling Joe it was okay for him to say his goodbyes now and fly home. So he did. But Joe's story had yet another level.

"Skip ahead a few years," he went on. "My dad had slipped into a coma and wasn't expected to live. It was February 1st. My brother and sisters and I believed he would die on February 14th, on our mother's birthday."

"And he did?"

He nodded. "But that's not all. I don't mean to be depressing here, but in 1975, I had an infant son who died suddenly of crib death. On the day my mother died, September 19th, it would have been my son's twenty-first birthday."

So here we have several synchronicities with dates and with spirit contact as Joe's mother and then his father were dying. And then there's the synchronicity for Trish. She and Rob were searching for more spirit contact stories to use in this book. The unplanned stop at the Apple store, the conversation with Joe, all *mirrored* the search. And the multilayered synchronicity perfectly illustrated the lengths to which spirits will go to communicate with their loved ones.

Look back through your own life. During major transitional periods, did events mirror other conditions in your life? If so, how?

UNUSUAL SYMBOLS

Anything can act as a symbol—that tree outside your window, a particular type of flower or bird, a song, seemingly random words on a billboard. But sometimes, the symbols that presage death and ultimately prove to be synchronistic are so unusual you miss the message until the death occurs.

Once a week, Trevor Simpson meets with a friend for their weekly meditation. At the end of the evening, they always draw a tarot card that usually provides insight on a pertinent issue. Trevor had just purchased a new tarot deck based on the poems and teachings of Rumi and was anxious to test it out. His friend went first and drew card number twenty, Judgment, but it was reversed. As he read the interpretation aloud, he sensed his friend wasn't finding it significant. Disappointed, he shuffled the seventy-four cards and drew a card for himself. It was the same card.

Trevor wrote it off to the fact that the deck was new, the card shiny, and dismissed the experience as meaningless. The next day, he heard about the death of a close friend. "After hearing the news of Charlie's death, I felt drawn to look at the cards again. The poem on the front of the card by Rumi read, 'By love, the dead are made living.' I think Charlie made one last appearance!"

Synchronicity and Pets

Many of us consider our animal companions to be members of our family. So when we get a new pet, it's like a birth—we celebrate, we call in the neighbors. And when a pet dies, we mourn.

In 2000, we bought our daughter Megan a dusky conure (a type of parrot) for her birthday and named her Kali. From the moment we brought her home, Kali got along famously with our golden retriever. Our three cats didn't seem to know what to make of her and never bothered her. Trish's dad, who was living with us then and in a wheelchair, got a real kick out of Kali when she rode on the back of his wheelchair or on his shoulder.

At first, she spent her days on our back porch, always out of her cage, where she could see other birds in the yard. Rob taught her to say a few words, which she eagerly used whenever one of us was within range.

As she got older, we moved her cage and its stand outside every morning, beneath a large schefflera tree. The tree had begun its life in Trish's parents' backyard, and when we moved, we dug up the tree and brought it with us. By the time Kali joined the family, the tree was five or six feet tall.

Her cage door was always open, and it wasn't long before she learned to climb onto the top of the cage, then into the tree. And it was her tree. When other birds came around, she made it clear that although they were welcome, she was the boss of this tree. She would climb down only when the spirit moved her to splash around in the large bowl we kept on top of her cage. Every evening at dusk, we moved her and the cage inside again. She would crawl inside her little hammock, roll onto her back, and sleep the night away. Kali was the paragon of "embrace the moment."

In September 2005, Trish's dad died. A month later, Hurricane Wilma roared into town. Fortunately, Wilma was traveling fast, but she was intense. The front part of the storm tore apart backyards, hurled fences apart, and ripped away power lines and roofs. The eye of the storm passed right over our area, and suddenly the sky turned blue, the air was balmy, the sun shone. We knew we had about thirty minutes to walk outside and assess the damage before the back side of the storm hit us.

The first thing we noticed was that Kali's tree had been split down the middle, the top of it lobbed off as if some monster had taken a huge bite out of it. It troubled us, but none of us voiced our concerns aloud. Since the tree had come from Trish's parents' yard and her father had passed away just a month earlier, she hoped its ruined state symbolized the closing of a chapter in her own life. There wasn't much time to dwell on it.

We cleaned up what we could and hurried inside as the back of the storm came at us.

Wilma moved on and a cold front swept in. No one had electricity, and all over the neighborhood generators chattered away. We put Kali outside near her tree, but it was apparent she wasn't happy about its ruined condition. Then something spooked her—a generator, one of us moving too quickly—and suddenly she took off into the dusk, squawking loudly.

We ran after her, thought we saw her perched on a pole, but then it got dark and she stopped squawking. We kept walking around the area, calling for her, but she didn't squawk back, didn't appear.

It got down into the 40s that night, and we worried about her out there in the cold. The next morning, Rob found her across the street, burrowed under some wet leaves, shivering. Not a single vet office was open. We just tried to keep her warm and coaxed her to drink water and eat. She died a day later.

The ruined tree was a warning about Kali's death. When we first opened the door and saw the tree, the three of us knew what it might mean but chose not to talk about it. It was as if we felt, at some collective level, that if we voiced our suspicions aloud, her death might come to pass. The fact that it would be unexpected and sudden was symbolized by what had happened to the tree. We've lived through numerous hurricanes in South Florida, but had never seen a tree split in two like this by wind and rain.

So, sometimes even when the symbol is obvious, we're reluctant to explore it. No one wants to think about the death of a favorite pet, but if you can watch for striking synchronicities related to your pet, you can prepare yourself for the inevitable day.

If your pet's habits change, if an event happens that damages or destroys your pet's favorite spot, if you feel unsettled by something with your pet, don't dismiss these events or feelings as meaningless. It may be that your pet or that enfolded order within the universe is trying to prepare you for your pet's demise.

More uplifting are synchronicities that appear after the death of a beloved animal. It's your pet telling you that all is well, and you and your animal friend will meet again.

Dreams That Presage Death

"The unconscious helps by communicating things to us . . . informing us of things which by all logic we could not possibly know," wrote Carl Jung in his autobiography, *Memories, Dreams, Reflections*.

Jung was referring to synchronistic phenomena, premonitions and dreams that come true.

In the chapter on life after death, Jung recounts a dream he had the night before his mother died. His description is harrowing and everything in the dream is excessive, of mythic proportions. The dense and ominous forest in which he found himself had huge trees, tremendous boulders. He heard a shrill, piercing whistle that seemed to reverberate through the entire cosmos, and it terrified him so badly that his knees shook. He heard wild crashing in the underbrush, and then a gigantic dog burst out. As it raced past Jung, he suddenly grasped what it was: a creature meant to carry away a human soul.

The next morning he received a call that his mother had died suddenly and unexpectedly.

Jung knew that the Wild Huntsman is an important god in mythology. At its root, this myth is about the Teutonic god Wotan or Odin, his Norse name. He used to speed through the night air on his eight-legged horse, followed by the spirits of the dead. Odin's Wild Ride, as his passage came to be called, nearly always presaged war, destruction, death. Jung points out that Wotan was also a nature spirit revived in the legend of Merlin and the Grail and became symbolic of the deep secret wisdom of the alchemists. "Thus the dream says that the soul of my mother was taken into the greater territory of the self which lies beyond the segment of Christian morality, taken into the wholeness of nature and spirit in which conflicts and contradictions are resolved."

Jung, of course, was steeped in knowledge about mythology, so it isn't surprising that his dream featured mythological figures and landscapes. But through the collective unconscious, common to all of us, your death dreams may also contain mythological elements. So if you encounter images or symbols with which you're not familiar, research them. Pick out the most startling symbol and do a search on the Internet. For example, if someone was devoured by a wolf in a dream, Google "wolf as symbol." You may discover that your unconscious is richer and more complex than you ever imagined.

Sometimes, dreams that predict death are shockingly direct. After returning from a writers' conference in late May 2000, Trish dreamed that she was still at the conference and someone handed her a yellow Post-it that read, "Your mother just passed away." Less than two weeks later, her mother died.

In between these two extremes are dreams that may hint at death, but don't provide enough clues for you to be sure. Perhaps these dreams are intended to nudge you toward closer scrutiny of your beliefs about life after death, free will, spirit communication, even reincarnation. The dreams may be encouraging you to explore the nature of reality through books, workshops, retreats, shamanic journeys, and the geography of your inner world. In other words, this type of death dream may be a symbolic representation of a kind of initiation, where you leave behind one type of lifestyle, worldview, relationship, and make the transition to something different and richer.

Other Predictive Signs

Your own questions can prompt an answer through synchronicity and a communication from spirits. Let's say you've been wondering whatever happened to that next-door neighbor you had when you were five. Then one day on Facebook you reconnect with people from your old neighborhood and discover your former neighbor died several years ago.

It's as if the act of asking the question sets forces in motion and the universe, spirits, or both get to work, bringing circumstances together so that your question is answered.

One day, Rebecca was thinking about neighbors she hadn't seen for forty years. They owned a large trucking company and their son used to play with Rebecca's younger brother. What had impressed her about these people was that they had come from moderate backgrounds but became quite wealthy because of their lucrative transport company. "That same day, I was browsing the obituaries and noticed the mother's name among the deceased."

The synchronicity here is that she was wondering about these people, then *just happened* to glance through the obituaries *on that very day* and found her answer. She felt the synchronicity was contact from the other side.

Not every synchronicity you experience indicates spirit contact, but some do, particularly if spirit communication is your focus and intention. Fluctuations in air temperature, unusual disturbances in the air, certain scents, and even glimpsing movement in the corner of your eye can be spirit contact. But most of us dismiss these incidents as imagination. During a visit to Cassadaga, a central Florida spiritualist community, we were in one of the gift shops and the clerk was ringing up our purchases. She suddenly brushed her fingertips across her cheeks and giggled.

"Oh, those spider-web sensations," she said. "I wish they wouldn't do that."

"What's that mean?" we asked.

"Spirit sometimes tickles my face. It feels like a spider web or feathers."

You might dismiss such subtle sensations as nothing but environmental factors, and that might be true. However, if a passing scent is familiar to you, bringing back a memory of an old friend's cologne, it could be a hint of spirit contact. That's especially true if you were recently thinking about or missing the person in question.

Pay attention to your environment, and if there are changes—scents, for instance, or objects that are rearranged in your home—take note of them. Spirit may be talking to you!

At the Moment of Death

"There is no separate, indivisible, specific point of death," wrote Jane Roberts in *Seth Speaks*. "Life is a state of becoming, and death is a part of this process of becoming." When you die, you don't really die. You simply become . . . well, something else, something grander, something beyond your wildest dreams. So in that space of the wildest dreams, as you're dying, your consciousness reaches out and touches the consciousness of someone you may or may not know who is receptive, who can hear or see you. Or it may touch an object that you know will be noticed by the living.

As her parents neared their twenty-second wedding anniversary, Sabrina's father was terminally ill with cancer. Knowing he was approaching death, he purchased a beautiful anniversary clock for Sabrina's mother. It had a glass dome over it, with pendulums inside that twirl around, back and forth in a circular motion. He gave the clock to her aunt to keep for her mother just in case he wasn't still there to give it to her. But he was, and on their twenty-second anniversary, he gave Sabrina's mother the anniversary clock, which she loved.

The clock kept perfect time, and was sitting on the fireplace mantle when, two weeks later, her father died. He was forty-two, and had died at 9:50 P.M. The next day, Sabrina and her family noticed that the hands of the clock were stopped at 9:50. Her grandfather tried to reset it, but the clock refused to run. "For several years after Dad's death, Mom took the clock to clockmakers, but no one could figure out how to keep it running, and it always stopped at 9:50. I inherited the clock when Mom died, and took it to a friend whose lifelong hobby has been making clocks. He couldn't get the clock to work." Today, Sabrina has the clock on a closet shelf, the hands frozen on 9:50. "None of the clock experts were ever able to explain why the mechanisms wouldn't work."

This story is one of the classics about synchronicity, spirit contact, and death: a clock stops at the moment of death and never moves again. The clock is taken to clock clinics, clock doctors, clock experts, and is deemed to be in perfect working condition, yet the hands remain frozen at the very time the individual died. Time has run out—that's the message.

How common is this experience? Well, check with Google. If you do a search for "clocks that stop when someone dies," nearly a million sites come up. This event is known as deathbed phenomena.

There are other types of deathbed phenomena. Recent research at King's College London found that 10 percent of terminally ill patients or their loved ones report some sort of inexplicable event. Dr. Peter Fenwick, an author and the neuro-psychiatrist who conducted the study, says there are three types of this phenomena: the dying are visited by loved ones who have already passed on, have visions of the afterlife, or are visited by a loved one they didn't know was dead. People who are with the dying patient may notice clocks or other digital and mechanical objects that stop working. Bells sometimes go off, animals react.

The symbols and synchronicities surrounding death are numerous. When Carl Jung died, a tree that he used to sit beneath was struck by lightning. This story was told to author Miguel Serrano by Jung's daughter. In instances like this, it's as if the spirit of the individual and the spirit of nature are coop-erating in some way to make a statement.

After Death

In Alice Sebold's novel *The Lovely Bones*, the young girl who is raped and murdered at the beginning of the story observes, from the afterlife, the effects of her death on her family and friends. The most we see of the afterlife is the playground where the protagonist usually is when she watches life on earth. But her emotions—grief, sadness, longing, loneliness for her previous life—are palpable. Although the book is fiction, it touches you in a way that drives home why spirits attempt communication with the living.

"The dead come calling for all the reasons that we visit each other in ordinary life," wrote Robert Moss in *The Dreamer's Book of the Dead.* "They come because they want to make up, or make out. They come because they are lonely, or in the mood for gossip, or because they want a drinking buddy. They come for closure and mutual forgiveness and blessing. They come to deal with their unfinished business and pay off their debts."

The dead also drop by to check on the people they knew and loved—they're curious, they want to help out. And as we've talked about in other chapters, they use whatever they can to make themselves known.

But it isn't just the spirits of people we love who communicate with us. Sometimes, a spirit that is unknown to us tries to communicate. The dead are often as idiosyncratic as the living, as this next story illustrates.

Greetings from the Other Side

When Trish was a sophomore in college, she worked part time for the lead pathologist in a hospital. Dr. Stowens hired Trish to develop and print photos of DNA, chromosomes, and other microscopic material harvested during autopsies. Her darkroom was in the basement of the hospital, accessible only through the morgue.

Many days when she walked into the morgue, a body would be on the table, awaiting autopsy. Sometimes it was covered; most of the time, it was not. It invariably startled her to see someone on the table, a man or woman whose life had reached the end and whose body would now be carved up in the name of science. It wasn't the physical body that disturbed her, but that the spirit had no physical home now.

So one afternoon when she was in the darkroom and only a door stood between her and a body awaiting an autopsy, she silently asked the spirit in the other room to communicate with her. This was years before digital photography, which meant she used negatives, an enlarger, and high-contrast photography paper, along with three or four trays filled with various chemicals. The dark room was sealed against light leaks. As she proceeded to develop the negatives, she kept thinking about the soul of the body in the other room. She made the enlargements and placed them into the appropriate trays.

When she glanced at the paper in the first tray, she realized something was wrong. The paper was black except in the middle, where two pale, foggy forms appeared. She removed the sheet from the tray, held it up to the safe light—then caught her breath and dropped it into the solution that stopped the image from developing any further. From here, it went into the fix solution that stabilized the image.

When she removed it from that solution and turned on the overhead light, she stared in amazement. The two images were letters: HI, the greeting scrawled across the center of the photo paper. She left the darkroom, drove to a photo store, and bought new chemicals, new photo paper, and went through the same process with the same negative. The results were identical.

She showed Dr. Stowens the images. He studied them in silence, his medical training seemingly battling his intuitive knowledge as a healer, a pathologist, and as a man who dealt daily with the dead. "It's a light leak," he said.

"C'mon," Trish said. "Since when do light leaks spell words?"

He just looked at her with his wide, dark eyes. "Go back to work, Trish. Get me some good prints of those chromosomes."

Trish felt he saw the same thing she did—a greeting from beyond—but it wasn't appropriate for a pathologist to dabble in spirit contact.

Pets Communicating after Death

One of the most common instances of synchronicity and spirit communication occurs with our animal companions who have passed on. Animals, like humans, use a variety of methods to contact us. They may come through a reading with a medium, or can make their presences known through sounds, dreams, visions. They'll use whatever is available to them.

Some years ago, Darren had a black and white cat named Sylvester, who was killed on the road outside his house. Darren and his family weren't home at the time, and the distraught woman who hit Sylvester moved him out of the road and put him in the yard. When Darren discovered the cat, he placed him in a box. The next morning, he started digging a grave in his backyard.

The ground was too rocky, so he headed for a forest a few miles away. He wanted to dig a hole that was deep enough to prevent wild animals from finding Sylvester. He had the local radio station playing in his car while he worked. When the hole was done, Darren said his goodbyes to Sylvester and placed the box in the hole. Just then, the radio started playing Peter Gabriel's *Digging in the Dirt.* "I was beside myself thinking of all the songs that could possibly come on the radio and how appropriate that it was this song. Now, whenever I hear that song, I think back to that day, when I said farewell to my little pal."

This kind of synchronicity and spirit contact is so *literal* that you wonder who or what is orchestrating events. But perhaps there's no single force or power behind such events.

Perhaps our ideas about the nature of consciousness are too narrow and should be re-evaluated.

Synchronicity and Death Delayed

Can death be delayed? This may sound like a strange question, but there do seem to be times when an individual suddenly chooses a different path. It's our free will at work, making new choices as a situation evolves.

When Harriet lived in Boston, she was close to a married couple, Dave and Joan. During the seven years they'd been married, Dave and Joan had been trying to conceive, but without success. One night in April 1970, Dave drove to a bar on the other side of the city and had too much to drink. On his way home, he was speeding, lost control of his Mustang on a dangerous curve, and rammed into a tree. Dave should have died. He broke numerous bones and was on a respirator. The accident happened at 2:02 A.M., April 13, 1970.

"When we received the call and went to the hospital, I found Joan in the hospital chapel, on her knees, sobbing, begging God to let Dave live because she wanted a baby so badly," says Harriet.

Dave not only survived, he had no aftereffects at all.

Within a year, Dave and Joan conceived and had a son. On April 12, 1972, Dave went to the *same bar* on the other side of Boston. Coming home after midnight, once again inebriated and driving too fast, he flew around the same dangerous curve and smashed into a steel utility pole. He was taken to the *same* hospital. He had sustained a closed head injury and it killed him.

According to the police report, the accident occurred at 2:02 A.M. on April 13, 1972, *exactly two years to the minute* from his first accident. In both accidents, the police knew the time because the car clocks had stopped at the moment of impact.

A sequence of events like this creates more questions than it answers. Did the universe answer Joan's sobbing supplications and allow Dave to survive another two years so that they could have their baby boy? Did Dave's soul decide at the last moment that it wasn't time yet to pass on? Whatever happened, the astonishing synchronicities point to a design much greater than we can imagine.

The dead speak to us in many ways, including synchronicities. So any time you feel you are experiencing spirit contact, look for the synchronicities—as guidance and confirmation that the universe really is far more mysterious and complex than we have been led to believe.

6

SPOOKS AND
SPIRITS

Mention contact with the other side, messages from deceased relatives, or spirit contact, and people often think of ghosts, in particular the kind of ghosts they've read about in books or seen in movies. You've probably heard stories that supposedly were real encounters with ghosts. Maybe you've had such an experience yourself. If so, you're in good company.

Lisa Rogak, author of *Haunted Heart: The Life and Times of Stephen King*, cited an account by Stephen King in which he found himself alone in a room with an apparition. He was getting ready to leave a political fundraiser and was digging through a pile of coats on a bed, looking for the ones belonging to him and his wife, Tabby. He realized someone was sitting in a chair across the room. King described him as bald, wearing glasses and a pinstripe suit. "I started to say something to him about how hard it was to find your coat at these things, and suddenly there was nobody there. The chair was empty."

A ghost can be described as a thought form projected from a spirit. It has no awareness, but performs a repetitive task. It's like a memory powerfully impressed within a specific location. It can continue for centuries, compulsively doing the same thing over and over again. It's harmless and can't exert any energy against living beings or inanimate objects. So, a ghost is nothing more than a spectral hologram of something or someone.

While a ghost has no awareness, spirits are the essences or souls of what we once were, human or animal. Spirits have freedom of motion and activity. An easy way to remember the difference is that a ghost is like a video or audio recording playing in an endless loop. A spirit seems aware of you and might be trying to communicate. Some are helpful, beneficial; others, not so much.

A haunting could be caused by a spirit who, for one reason or another, is trapped and either can't or won't move on. Such spirits are neither here nor there, and are capable of creating all kinds of phenomena. Fear is a major reason spirits get stuck between worlds.

Your First Encounter

There are no right or wrong answers in this activity. It's just a means of helping you focus on your feelings about these experiences.

1. If you encountered a ghost or spirit, how do you think you would react?

   a. I would be terrified.
   b. I would be thrilled.
   c. I would look for a logical explanation.
   d. My reaction would depend on what I was facing.
   e. After my initial surprise, I would try to confront the entity and tell it to move on.

2. How would you act in the aftermath of your encounter?

   a. I would tell everyone I know about it. I would even tell strangers!
   b. I wouldn't tell anyone. Best to keep quiet about this stuff.
   c. I might tell some of my friends about it, but not others.
   d. I would vow to never return to that place.
   e. I would gather friends and organize a ghost hunt.
   f. Maybe I would go back, maybe not.

Answer Key

If you answered C or D to question 1, then you're a potential ghost hunter. Regarding the other choices, whether you would be thrilled or terrified depends on the nature of the encounter. If it was your first such experience, it wouldn't be a good idea to attempt to confront an entity, unless you were with a group of experienced ghost hunters.

If you answered C, E, or F to question 2, you're also a potential explorer in this realm. If you chose B or D, you probably wouldn't want to pursue the matter. However, if you chose A, you're overly enthusiastic, and probably don't have the right temperament for ghost hunting. You need to stay calm and in control when making contact.

Previous Encounters with Ghosts

If you've already encountered a ghost or spirit, consider these questions about your experience:

- How did the encounter manifest? Was it an image, a voice, sounds, smells? Was there a change in temperature?
- What was your reaction? Were you frightened, excited, calm, or energized?
- Did you sense any emotions from the entity?
- Can you remember how you felt?
- Were you able to communicate with the entity?
- Were there any synchronicities related to your experience?

Keep track of your reactions. If you're having repeated encounters, notice how your reaction and the interactions change over time. If you're experiencing these encounters alone, ask someone else to join you. Get other opinions on what is going on. Be aware of deception that could be coming from maleficent or mischievous spirits. Back off if the encounters aren't positive. But as we discovered, sometimes that's impossible.

The Spiritualist Hotel

Nearly fifty years after the Fox sisters heard the mysterious rappings, medium George Colby founded the Cassadaga Spiritualist Camp in central Florida. Today, it's a flourishing community just north of Disney World. Most of the residents are mediums and psychics who speak to the dead. (You can read more about spiritualist communities in Chapter 7.) But you don't have to be a medium to experience contact with spirits, as we found in a visit years ago.

It was a chilly day when we checked into our lodgings in Cassadaga with our infant daughter. Oddly enough, we were the only guests. We had our choice of rooms and selected one on the second floor that provided a view of the camp. When we entered the hotel after dinner, we were struck by how eerily quiet it was. Since the hotel didn't have an elevator, we folded up Megan's stroller and headed up the stairs to the second floor. It was so still, the groaning and creaking of the steps and the old wooden floors sounded abnormally loud.

We settled in for the evening with our books, and didn't bother locking the door. The town was deserted, the hotel was empty; what was the point? Just before midnight, Trish got up to scour the closet for additional blankets, found one, and climbed back into bed. Megan had fallen asleep earlier. We were still awake, reading, when we heard loud clunking footfalls in the hallway. The stomping grew louder, moving down the hall toward our room.

Rob leaped out of bed and hurried to the door. As he put his hand on the doorknob to open it, a feeling of dread overwhelmed him. The thuds now sounded preternatural, echoing down the hall like something out of *The Shining*, something coming from another dimension, so hard and loud it felt as if the floor was shaking. Trish moved Megan, still asleep, to our bed and hurried over to Rob, who was locking the door.

"What the hell is it?" she hissed.

"Not the night clerk." He pressed his ear to the door.

As the clunks and thuds continued moving in our direction, a profound sense of malevolence electrified the air. For moments, neither of us moved. Then the thuds stopped. Total silence. Yet, we felt a presence right outside our door.

Without saying a word, we immediately shoved a heavy wooden dresser in front of one door and moved the bed in which Megan had been sleeping in front of the other door. We didn't know what we would do if whatever was on the other side of the door moved through the door and barrier we'd erected. We waited, and gradually the feeling of terror dissipated. We knew it was over.

The next morning when we checked out, we asked the manager if the hotel was haunted. He nodded. "But only by friendly spirits." Now, years later, the hotel's website says the same thing. *Friendly spirits*. Maybe the one we met was just visiting.

If You See a Ghost or Spirit

If you see or sense a spirit and don't feel threatened by it or uncomfortable with what you're seeing, follow these simple guidelines:

- Relax and take note of as many details as possible. If you can see the ghost, what does it look like? Is it male or female? Is the clothing unusual in some way? What is the entity doing?

- Engage your senses. What do you hear? Is there a scent of any kind? If it's a familiar spirit—a deceased loved one— there might be smells, a particular perfume or maybe cigar smoke that you associate with that person. The scent isn't always from someone you knew, though. While touring the Biltmore estate in Asheville, North Carolina, we continually caught the scent of pipe tobacco. You couldn't smoke inside the building, so at the end of the tour, we asked one of the guides if the Biltmore was haunted and told him what we'd smelled. The man smiled. "The night shift guards smell it all the time."
- What synchronicities are associated with the experience?
- Address the entity out loud or silently. Ask what it wants.
- Regardless of where and when the contact occurs—a dream, vision, or altered state—be sure to record it once it's over. In your heightened state, the details may slip away from you too easily.
- If at any time you feel threatened, laugh. A spirit that is malicious or intends you harm can't sustain itself when you're laughing.
- Once you experience the contact, tell the entity it is free to leave and move on in its journey.

Psychic Protection

If you plan to visit a place that's known for being haunted or find yourself in such a place—either intentionally or not— it's a good idea to create a psychic shield to protect yourself against unwanted influences. Symptoms that could be related to the projection of negative energy toward you might include insomnia, disrupted sleep, nightmares, lower energy levels, or chronic fatigue.

These attacks can come from a living human, a maleficent spirit, or, oddly enough, a combination of the two.

The latter is what may have happened to us when a particularly aggressive and caustic individual came on our blog after we posted a story by one of our readers about a dramatic UFO sighting. The attacker, who wrote as Anonymous, belittled the story in such a demeaning manner that others came to the writer's defense. Anonymous seemed to thrive on the discord, which went on for dozens of comments.

Finally, after several days of increasingly hostile comments, Rob told Anonymous that any future comments would be deleted.

At the time, we were staying in a house in Cedar Key, Florida, located on the Gulf Coast, southwest of Gainesville. Rob had no sooner sat down to write the comment than his chair started sliding back and forth on its wheels, boxes on a shelf in a nearby walk-in closet rattled against each other, and Noah, our dog, lying a few feet from Rob, rocked back and forth as if he were in a hammock.

In the next room, the table where Trish was working started moving, stuff rattling on top of it. Our first thought: earthquake. It lasted seven or eight seconds and was followed by two or three milder "aftershocks" over the next twenty minutes.

Trish, who had been attempting to find the location of the obnoxious writer at the time of the incident, checked with an earthquake-monitoring site and found no mention of an earthquake on the Gulf Coast of Florida. Earthquakes are extremely rare in Florida since there aren't any fault lines. We checked with our daughter and her boyfriend, who were in another part of the house, but neither of them had noticed anything unusual. Later, when we went out to dinner, we asked several people about it. No one had felt anything.

Rob proceeded to write his comment, as planned. About the same time he posted it, another comment appeared suggesting that the harassing comments by Anonymous should be blocked or removed. When we humorously informed the writer about the "supernatural earthquake," she quickly wrote back to tell us that when she started to write her comment, she suddenly experienced a piercing headache and her dog threw up for no apparent reason. "There's a possibility that there's an entity with this person, a malefic spirit, who's creating all this havoc."

Of course, we don't know that for certain, but it was a synchronicity. Whatever the cause, we experienced a shaking just as Rob was about to put a stop to Anonymous's vitriolic attacks. Indeed, Anonymous responded angrily when he found out his comments would be deleted.

Afterward, as a precaution against future disturbances, we invoked psychic protection. You can adapt the following methods to fit your situation.

The Light of Protection

Settle into your favorite private place, in a comfortable chair, where no one will interrupt you for at least ten minutes. Take several deep breaths. As you exhale, feel yourself relaxing more and more deeply. Let your breath soften as you visualize a ball of white light surrounding you; it will block any negative energy before it can touch you. Make sure it extends about a foot away from your body, including your feet. Think of the luminous ball of light as a defense against any energy that might be exerted against you.

Focus on the light surrounding you. Rest assured that after you come out of your relaxed state, the bubble of light will remain with you for however long you need it. Any negative, invasive energy that comes your way will simply pass by you like wind moving around a barrier. Enjoy the certainty that you're protected and nothing but positive energy can come your way.

Religious Protection

One day Trish came home from the grocery store with another technique for psychic protection that she'd heard from a Cuban woman who often bags her groceries. Marina was a physician before she fled her homeland, and since she doesn't speak English well and isn't licensed to practice medicine in the United States, she took a minimum-wage job. When Trish mentioned the book we were working on, Marina looked startled, then proceeded to tell her of a ghostly encounter she'd experienced the night before and how she'd protected herself from a distraught spirit.

Marina was alone in her condominium, sleeping, when she abruptly awakened to the sound of a woman groaning and weeping, as if in great pain. Marina was certain the sound was coming from her bedroom and not from another condo. "The spirit was right there with me, next to me in bed, and I was terrified."

She immediately realized she needed to protect herself from psychic invasion and remembered a method she'd learned from a spiritualist in Cuba. She took a wooden cross from her night-stand, plunged it into a clear glass filled with water, and recited the Lord's Prayer. Just as she finished, her husband came home and turned on the lights, ending the frightful haunting.

Linda, who is Jewish, wrote to us on our blog after we posted Marina's story and said that for her, the Shema—an important part of the prayer service in Judaism—works well for general protection against negative influences of any kind. "I say only the first two lines, first in Hebrew and then in English, simply because I never memorized the rest of it. But even the first line—*Hear, O Israel: the Lord is our God, the Lord is one*—in Hebrew seems to create an instant globe of white light around you that shuts out negative energies."

Other Methods of Protection

When we posted that story on our blog, several people commented on how they protect themselves. Connie Cannon calls her home, St. Augustine, Florida, one of the most haunted cities in America. She has investigated hauntings and explored all types of spirit contact. For psychic protection in her mystical endeavors, she turns to the spirit world.

"My primary source of protection is to immediately call in every discarnate healer and protector who surrounds my life, those whose names I know and some whose names I don't know." She then asks for communication only with those entities, energies, and beings who are filled with light and love. Her request is followed by a sense of calmness and an awareness of complete and utter safety. Nearly always, there's an exquisite fragrance. "It's a psychic fragrance, profound, and envelops me with a sense of absolute comfort and removes all fears."

Natalie Thomas, a medium in New South Wales, Australia, calls on the Archangel Michael to envelope and protect her with his wings. "I ask that all guides and unseen helpers who are only of the light come forward with the highest vibration for me and my client. I ask that all blocks and negativity be removed, in all directions of time and space, and I tell them I love them and appreciate their help. Then I say the Lord's Prayer. When the client comes into my room, I ask permission to do the same thing for him or her."

But you don't have to be a psychic or medium in order to invoke psychic protection. You can follow any of these methods, adjust them to your own personal tastes and spiritual beliefs, or create your own.

Also, be alert for synchronicities that may help you fine-tune your invocations for protection. If, for instance, you're trying to create a protective shield around yourself and recently passed a car with a license plate that said "prayer" on it, then use prayer. In other words, follow the signs and symbols!

Sending Them on Their Way

If you think your house or someone else's is haunted, you can take action to get the lost spirit moving. Instead of thinking that you're dealing with someone strange and scary, consider the lost spirit to be a consciousness without a body that's attached to the world of the living and specifically to a particular location.

Don't accept spirits as unique houseguests. A lost spirit who haunts a residence doesn't belong there and needs to move on. The first thing you should do is simply tell the spirit to leave. Be firm, but courteous. Reassure lost spirits that there is no reason for fear; they're not going to hell.

If that doesn't work, be more forceful. It doesn't mean you should tell them to go to hell, but you should demand that they leave immediately. Make sure you believe what you're saying. Avoid any ambivalence. Don't harbor regrets. Some people find it intriguing to have a haunting, but it's not in your best interest—nor in the spirit's.

Another approach you can take is to call on guides for help, both yours and the trapped spirit's guides. This can be done through prayer or by simply asking your guides—aloud or silently—to help. There's more information on spirit guides in Chapter 12.

If these methods aren't effective, you can pursue a more material-oriented approach by altering the appearance of your residence. Painting the walls, moving the furniture, knocking out a wall, or adding a room could make your abode less appealing for a reticent spirit. But don't do this unless you really want to make the changes.

The Way of Orbs

One evening, during a spectacular sunset in south Florida, the atmosphere turned a reddish hue. Our daughter Megan, who was in high school, called our attention to the sky. Using a digital camera, we took several photos of her in our backyard and most were speckled with orbs—balls of light. It made for fascinating photos—the red sky decorated with orbs like Christmas decorations on an invisible pine tree.

It was fun to think that our backyard was full of spirits, sprites, and fairies, but the humidity was high and the orbs were probably moisture in the air or dust particles the camera picked up. In other words, not all orb photographs are captured images of spirit beings. People who are experienced in taking and analyzing orb photos can easily distinguish those related to atmospheric conditions from real ones that seem to represent a form of conscious energy. Those experts who have taken thousands of photos of orbs with high quality equipment and under conditions free of atmospheric interference are convinced that orbs represent spirits.

Typically, orbs are invisible to the eye, which is why orb hunters try to photograph them. But there have been numerous reports of individuals who have seen them. They've been spotted and videotaped, for instance, as they move above fields just prior to the appearance of a crop circle. C. Norman Shealy, an MD, speculates that, "orbs may be to the atmosphere what crop circles are to the earth." They've also been seen before, during, and after UFO sightings, and by individuals who have recently lost loved ones.

Karen A. recalls a variety of contacts with her husband in the months and years after his death in an auto accident. "One night, I was reading in my room when an orb the size of a tennis ball appeared above my bed," she wrote on her blog, Maggie's Garden. "It just hovered there for most of an hour, moving only slightly. Then it dimmed out like a light bulb. I searched for every possibility of what it could have been, but I know in my gut, I truly believe, it was spirit contact."

After Terri Patrick's mother died, she and her family had a number of experiences they believed were her mother's attempt to communicate with them: ringing phones with no number or connection; blinking lights; volume shifts on stereos; issues with the water temperature in the shower; voices; and tremendous orbs that appeared in photos. "While we all knew it was spirit contact, none of us felt any fear either," Terri said. "The most notable orb was in a picture taken of our youngest, the night of her junior prom. It was the night before my mother's wake. The orb in the picture was huge, almost the size of my daughter's head, right over her shoulder. It was very clear and defined."

Both Karen and Terri were comforted by the appearance of these orbs, and felt certain they were the spirits of deceased family members. If you experience a contact like this, it's wise to take stock of your feelings at the moment the incident occurs. We are all intuitive beings, and if you strongly sense that the orb is the spirit of your deceased loved one, then it probably is. Never deny the validity of your own experiences and perceptions just because an experience is unfamiliar to you or strange.

Orbs have entered public awareness more in the last decade. In fact, in Cassadaga, there's an orb tour every Saturday night. Some people do see orbs and photograph them on these tours. One evening, during a visit to Cassadaga, we met a woman on the porch of the Cassadaga Hotel who taught photography at the University of Miami and had come to town specifically to photograph orbs. She'd never captured one in a photo and hoped to do so on the orb tour. Just before the tour set off, it began to mist, and the professor immediately abandoned her plans. She later explained that the mist would create atmospheric conditions conducive to false orbs. So be aware of the weather if you're trying to photograph orbs.

Catching Orbs

If you've decided you want to photograph orbs, there are several preparatory steps you should take.

1. First, be serious about it. Decide that you'll dedicate a certain amount of time each week to your efforts. Make a list of possible locations. Maybe you know of a house or building that is said to be haunted. If it's a private home, you'll need permission to photograph on the property or inside the house. Cemeteries are another option. Visit during the day when the cemetery is open. Old public buildings—like an historic courthouse—are another possibility. Courthouses were once places where

people were hanged. Go during a time when others will be present.

2. Take a few minutes to meditate before you set out on your adventure. Focus on your intention that orbs will appear. Ask for guidance and reaffirm your intent.

3. Avoid taking someone with you who considers it a silly thing to do.

4. Point your camera toward a person or a group, since orbs seem attracted to people.

5. Avoid shooting outdoors on rainy days, even if the rain has stopped. Stay away from places that are dusty or where pollen or tiny insects might be in the air. Avoid using a flash, which might pick up dust or water particles in the air.

6. Use your intuition and find a method that works for you. If you don't get results, try again later. Or find a new location.

7. When the orbs start to appear, recall the steps you took that attracted the orbs. Next time, try the same method. Be willing to go back repeatedly.

Ghost Ship

Over time, certain ghost stories take on an archetypal nature. They transcend personal encounters and become archetypes, urban legends that help shape the nature of the location. That's particularly true when a sighting involves an isolated locale, like an island. In southern Chile, one such legend involving a famed ghost ship has become part of the mythological roots of the island of Chiloe.

It was a synchronicity that led us to Chiloe and the legend of the ghost ship *Caleuche*. We first heard about it on a flight from Miami to Santiago, in July 1983. We were on our honeymoon and Chile was our first destination. We struck up a conversation with the woman who sat next to us and asked where the mythology, the mystery, of Chile could be found.

"Chiloe," she said without hesitation.

We'd never heard of it.

She explained it was an island off Puerto Montt, where land transportation ended in southern Chile. From Puerto Montt, you had to take a ferry to Chiloe. The ghost ship legend of the *Caleuche,* she said, was deeply ingrained in islanders. The ship was supposedly manned by sorcerers, or *brujos*, who were immortal and possessed the power to alter their shapes at will. They could transform themselves into wolves, fish, rocks, and birds, and when they took human form, they were tall, foreign, blond. Even the ship was believed to be able to transform its shape.

We were hooked. Our synchronistic choice of seats pretty much defined our journey through Chile. We spent two days in Santiago, then boarded an overnight train to Puerto Montt. It was the middle of winter in Chile, and as soon as we arrived in Puerto Montt, we went shopping for jackets. Floridians are never prepared for winter—especially in July! The next morning, we hopped the ferry to Ancud, one of three towns on Chiloe. Once we found a place to stay, we started our exploration.

At a local restaurant, we quickly discovered that the ghost ship wasn't just a myth to the locals. It was based on real events that involved encounters with the *brujos*—witches, evil ghosts—who supposedly crewed the ship. The villagers also spoke of the *pincoyas*—the mermaids—that inhabited the waters around the island. Everything in the restaurant, from the ashtrays to the art on the walls, depicted the ship, the mermaids, the *brujos*.

Our waiter directed us to a neighborhood down the road, where many of the homes were built on stilts that keep them above the water. "Ask anyone you see about the *Caleuche*."

We walked into the neighborhood the waiter had indicated and asked the people we saw out and about if they knew anyone who had had an experience with the *Caleuche*. We were directed to one of the stilted homes, climbed the rickety steps, and rapped at the weathered wooden door. An elderly woman with hunched shoulders and tragic eyes peered out.

Trish, who speaks Spanish, explained that we were writers researching a magazine story about the *Caleuche*. We understood that she had had an experience and could we talk to her for a few minutes? She stepped outside, into the bright, chilly air. In a crisp, lyrical Spanish, she said, "I was very young. My mother and I were on our way over the bridge." She pointed at the bridge we had just crossed, which spans the Rio Pudeto and overlooks the harbor where the *Caleuche* had been sighted over the decades. "It was dusk. I had a pebble in my shoe and had to stop to shake it out. When I looked up, I saw it."

"Saw what?" Trish asked.

"The ship," she whispered. "First I saw the bright lights shining in the dusk. Then a mast and another mast, and then the sails, filled with wind. The boat was huge. I heard music. It was beautiful, seductive, beyond description. Like I said, I was young, just ten, not old enough to be afraid. But the sight terrified my mother. She knew about the ghosts—the *brujos*—about the abductions, how men had disappeared and returned years later, profoundly changed. She grabbed my hand and we ran."

Abductions. Evil ghosts. Trish pressed her for more information, but she shook her head. "I have said enough. It is not safe to talk about such things. And you must not write about what I have told you for many years. Until I am dead."

With that, she slipped back into her little house on stilts and we stood there, looking at each other. We later wrote a long article about the *Caleuche* and our experiences for *Fate* magazine. But because the woman had asked us not to write about what she'd told us "for many years," we didn't include it. But it's now been twenty-eight years and we suspect the elderly woman is long dead.

The *Caleuche* story illustrates that beliefs about hauntings are as endemic to other cultures as they are to our own. It also shows how the power of belief—in this case, a belief that might be labeled as superstition—becomes an archetype for the people who inhabit a particular area and may predispose them to experience the essence of that belief.

Haunted House

No chapter on hauntings would be complete without at least one story of a haunted house. This one is fascinating for its colorful location, the history of the house, and the identity of the prominent ghost.

Located on Skirrid Mountain near Abergavenny, Wales, the house is a medieval manor with original interior walls, including a huge fireplace. The kitchen was once a barn and still has the old cobbled floor and a urine trough down one side. Carved upon the original beam above the dining room door are a fox, deer, hare, bird, and a six-petal design associated with witches. The house was known as a stopping-off place for drovers, who took animals from Wales to London across the mountains to avoid paying tolls on the roads. Medieval drovers were known as masters of mystery and magic.

The house was vacant for decades. A few years ago, a friend of the medium and healer Jane Clifford bought the place despite Jane's advice to look elsewhere. Jane clearly remembers her first visit. "Upon arriving with my son, I got out of the car by a barn and immediately felt a tragedy of some kind. I didn't tell my friend. After all, she had to live there alone."

On her next visit, her friend, who we'll call Maude, said she had seen ghosts near the barn. Inside the house, Jane picked up something on the medieval past. She sensed tremendous occult magical power there, as though the house were some sort of portal, where the veil between the world and time was particularly thin. After just one night there, Jane felt psychically shocked for over a week and so did her twenty-two-year-old son, who was well-grounded and didn't scare easily.

In the fall of 2009, she reluctantly returned to the house to see Maude. While looking out of a window at the magnificent view of the mountain, Jane felt a male spirit nearby. She felt as if she were seeing the view through his eyes or as if he were seeing it again through her eyes.

A voice in her head said, "It wasn't so bad being held here compared to what came later. This wonderful view reminded me of my homeland."

A memory of a visit to the Bavarian mountains came to mind. Jane gathered that his homeland was Bavaria and that he had been a German POW, an important one. A mini movie played in Jane's mind: wartime cars pulled up in the dark outside the house and from these vehicles emerged military men in great coats, and other men in trilby hats and overcoats. She felt a great sense of secrecy. Churchill came to mind. She sensed that decisions were made in the house that affected the history of the country.

The next day, Jane asked Maude if she knew anything of the history of the house. Maude only knew that the military had used it until the 1950s, then it had been vacant until she'd bought it.

During the summer of 2010, Jane went to a party near her home, two hours from the haunted house, where she met two couples who lived on the same side of Skirrid Mountain as the house in question. When Jane mentioned Maude's house, one of the women said she knew it well and added that Rudolf Hess was held there by British forces, and was often seen by locals walking about the property. Jane says, "You can imagine my shock that I had been communicating with the ghost of the third most powerful Nazi in Germany!"

In fact, Hess had defected in the war, dropped by parachute into Scotland, and tryed to broker an end to the war. From 1942–45, he was held as a prisoner in Wales, part of the time in the Abergavenny Military Hospital, located near Maude's house. Even though the house isn't mentioned in the history of Hess in Wales, Jane is convinced he stayed there, that top-level secret meetings were held in the house, and information was given to the British that affected the outcome of the war.

Churchill didn't want Hess tried for war crimes, believing he had exonerated himself by defecting and providing valuable information. However, Stalin insisted Hess stand trial. He was found guilty and imprisoned at Spandau, Berlin, where he died at the age of 93.

"It's hard to describe what occurs to me in that house," Jane says. "It's as if there were a tear in the fabric of space and time. I have stayed in many castles in Wales, but none has affected me this way."

Identifying a Spirit

Not everyone has Jane's intuitive talents, but there are other ways of identifying a spirit or ghost inhabiting a house.

1. Decide if there's a personal connection. Did someone you know, family member or friend, die recently? If so, would that person have reason to attract your attention from the afterlife? Were there unfinished issues? Could the spirit have a message for you, possibly a warning?
2. If no one comes to mind, pay attention to what the spirit does. If it's a repetitive action, it might be a harmless ghost—a memory embedded in the environment that lacks awareness. Does the spirit give you any clues to its identity?
3. Did anyone die in the house before you moved there? Check public records to find the names of former residents. Talk to elderly neighbors. Find out if other residents complained of a ghostly presence.
4. If all else fails, ask the spirit for clues. Look for synchronicities, such as an encounter with a former neighbor who might know something that leads to the identity of the spirit.

If you're able to identify the spirit haunting a residence or building, you probably have a better idea why it's haunting this particular location. Maybe he or she lived there for decades and remains fond of the house. Maybe the spirit is looking for something or someone. Maybe it simply wants someone to identify it before moving on. Whatever it is, wish the spirit well and send it on its way. As stated earlier, avoid any attempt to keep a spirit around as a "mascot" from the other side. That will only interfere with the spirit's journey and could result in unwanted spooky events.

7

THE MEDIUM AND
THE MESSAGE

The entertainment world of TV and movies primes our collective consciousness in a unique way. We can vicariously experience anything screenwriters can imagine. Love, sex, birth, death, intrigue, comedy, the supernatural: movies and TV shows dish it out and we gobble it up. But on a deeper level, these stories help to make us more receptive to new beliefs.

Think back for a moment to shows like *The X-Files*, *The 4400*, *The Event*, and *V*. Are they preparing us for contact? What about movies like *The Sixth Sense*, *Dead Again*, and *Hereafter*? Do they urge us to think more deeply about life after death, spirit contact, and reincarnation? Do they open our minds to new possibilities? Over time, because of TV shows and movies, a tipping point is reached on certain ideas and they are more readily accepted into the mainstream.

In June 2000, the SyFy channel began airing *Crossing Over*, a show hosted by medium John Edward. The format was simple. Edward read for people in his audience, most of whom had lost loved ones and were seeking contact. His book by the same name provides great insight into what it's like to be a medium. He talks about the sometimes-bumpy journey that led him to television, bestselling books, and his celebrity status. By 1995, his guides were encouraging him to put more time and effort into his psychic work, but Edward felt insecure about how he might be perceived. He could just imagine people asking what he did for a living: "Oh, I talk to dead people." Even worse, he would have to put "psychic medium" on his tax return.

Edward, however, followed the advice of his guides and became a psychic celebrity. No longer on TV, he holds seminars all over the world, does small group reading sessions, and private readings.

PAYING FOR READINGS

Before you rush to John Edward's website to schedule a reading, however, consider the price: $750.

There are plenty of psychics and mediums who are just as accurate as Edward, but lack his media status, so they can't charge that kind of money for a reading—at least, not if they hope to make a living. Keep in mind that a higher fee for a reading doesn't necessarily guarantee a more satisfying or accurate result. For most mediums, a reading should cost between $1–$2 a minute.

One of the best readings we ever had was with a West Virginia psychic, Millie Gemondo, who at that time charged $35 a reading. We also paid $150 for a reading from a French-Canadian psychic who was accurate, but lacked social skills—she didn't have a clue how to present devastating information in a humane manner.

However, psychics and mediums, like anyone else who performs a service, deserve compensation. It's up to you how much that service is worth. So if you believe that money equals value, then by all means lay out $750 for a reading from John Edward, Sylvia Browne, James Van Praagh, or any other media figure. But if you run into a psychic medium on a flight, do not ask how your Aunt Bertha is doing on the other side, okay?

Mediums Versus Psychics

Mediums talk to the dead. When they use tools—cards, stones, crystals, whatever—the tool is generally used to get focused or to tune in on the client. Their focus is to receive information from spirits.

A reading may begin with the medium providing names of the spirits around you who are eager to communicate with you, presumably family members and friends who have passed on. Some mediums might get full names immediately, but more than likely the medium provides initials or repeats a string of names that start with the same letter—Joe or Jack, for instance. The gender of the spirit is usually apparent. If a name is familiar to you, then the medium imparts a message from the spirit.

Usually, a medium doesn't provide information about the future unless the spirit knows something about what's coming up for you. This is one area where mediums and psychics usually differ. People who go to mediums hope to contact their deceased loved ones; people who go to psychics tend to be more interested in their current relationships, jobs, families, and what lies in the future.

However, there are crossovers. Millie Gemondo, the psychic from West Virginia whom we mentioned earlier, sometimes receives messages from spirits, but doesn't consider herself a medium.

Hazel Burley, a medium who lives in Cassadaga, Florida, a town of mediums, is strictly a medium, but occasionally provides predictions if she's given the information from spirits.

Psychics generally use tools—tarot cards, your palm, a personal belonging like a piece of jewelry, regular playing cards, stones, crystals, tea leaves—but not always. Some psychics simply enter a kind of meditative state, their "zone," and start talking. Others read your aura or energy field. Every psychic has a particular method and what works for one may not work for another. Millie Gemondo, for example, uses a deck of regular playing cards, but it's obvious she isn't reading them.

During one reading some years ago, she warned Rob to be careful while windsurfing, that he might injure his foot. We asked which card had yielded that information. "The two of clubs," she said with a laugh, and tapped her temple. A month later, Rob was windsurfing at a local lake, came into shore, leaped off the board—and onto a broken beer bottle. He ended up in the ER.

Later in the chapter, we talk to several mediums who provide information on how they work with spirits to obtain information. In the meantime, here are some parameters for readings with mediums and psychics that should help you obtain the best reading possible.

- Reveal nothing about yourself. If the medium or psychic provides a name or information that resonates for you, just keep listening and taking notes. Don't reveal that the information is accurate unless the medium/psychic asks. Sometimes they do ask to verify if they're on the right track.
- Watch for synchronicities related to your reading. Perhaps, earlier that day, you thought of your grandmother, how much you miss her, and the first name the medium picks up is that of your grandmother. Or perhaps the medium describes the way a particular spirit died and the description fits your grandmother's death. Mediums and psychics also pick up on the animal spirits around you. Some years ago, novelist Nancy Pickard had a reading with medium Hazel Burley in Cassadaga. Hazel described a white poodle that was around her. Nancy had lost a poodle that she adored, so this mention of the dog confirmed that Hazel was tuning in on her.
- If a medium tells you that you have an Indian guide, be skeptical. While you may actually have an Indian guide, our experience has been that the phrase is a generic term that some mediums fall back on when they aren't picking up anything.
- If you're concerned that a medium or psychic is going to predict your death, tell the person at the outset that you don't want to know that information. In all likelihood, the medium or psychic won't know that answer anyhow.
- Have your questions prepared before the reading starts. Write them down. Focus on them for a few minutes

before the reading begins. It should help you obtain a clear reading.

- If a medium or psychic says she needs an additional payment to remove a curse or to cast a spell to manifest your fondest wish, don't do it. This may seem like obvious advice, but sometimes when a medium makes a direct hit, people become gullible and will fall for such crass gimmicks.

How to Find a Good Medium or Psychic

Decide what you want to know and who could answer it best—a psychic or a medium. Then begin your search.

The best way to find a medium or a psychic is through recommendations by people you know. Again, this may seem obvious, but a referral from someone you know who had a positive experience is far preferable than trying a psychic.com website or an 800-PSYCHIC phone line. If you don't know anyone who has had a reading by a psychic or medium, then poke around on blogs and websites about the paranormal. You're sure to find leads.

Select five or six names. Then let synchronicity guide you to the right individual. Perhaps one of the people on your list has an unusual name that has recurred throughout your life and you always have positive experiences with people who have this name. That in itself might be the nudge you need to pick that individual.

Or perhaps someone on your list has a phone number that is nearly identical to yours. Or maybe their numerical address or the name of the street on which they live corresponds to positive or negative addresses in your own life. In other words, look for the signs.

If there's a New Age or metaphysical bookstore in your area, you should be able to find a psychic or medium easily. Many of these bookstores have individuals who do readings in the store.

If you still can't find someone, then perhaps it's time to take a trip to San Francisco, Taos, Sedona—or to one of the two spiritualist communities in the United States, where psychics and mediums abound.

Finding Guidance at Spiritualist Sites

Since there are only two spiritualist communities in the United States, here's what we know about them and why you may want to travel to these places for a reading.

Cassadaga, Florida

Orlando is known for Disney World. Thrilling rides, visions of tomorrow, theme parks that rival each other. But just half an hour north, at the end of a lonely road through dense pine forests, lies another kind of world, where the residents speak to the dead on a daily basis.

Cassadaga, Florida, has existed in some form since the heyday of spiritualism. Back in the 1800s, George Colby, a medium from Pike, New York, was directed by his spirit guide, Seneca, to establish a spiritualist camp in the south. He ended up in central Florida, which was mostly swamps and mangroves, and proceeded to set up a community. On December 18, 1894, the Cassadaga Spiritualist camp was officially chartered.

Today, the camp consists of fifty-seven acres with fifty-five homes, two lakes (Colby Lake and Spirit Lake), a haunted hotel, a bookstore, gift shops, and a host of mediums and psychics. Walk around the quiet streets in town and you'll notice that many houses have signs out front that read, "Reverend So and So—Medium." So if you've come for a reading with a medium, this is the place to be.

But even here, discretion is in order. In 1931, the camp association required that all mediums who worked on the grounds of the camp had to be registered with the association. Presumably, those who were approved were considered valid mediums. Other mediums or psychics, practicing outside the camp, were supposedly questionable and might use tarot cards and astrology. As a result, a schism developed over the years and continues today, an ongoing dispute between the "inside" mediums and the "outside" practitioners.

The Cassadaga Hotel is located on the border of the camp. Across the street, the readers are considered outsiders. From our experience, you can obtain excellent or humdrum readings on either side.

The hotel and the bookstore across the street maintain lists of mediums available on any given day for readings. Or you can walk around the camp or along the shops on the other side of the road and let your intuition guide you to the right individual. In nearby Lake Helen, more mediums and psychics can be found. Psychics are available there, and the store also offers a variety of workshops.

As of late fall 2010, prices for a reading on either side of the road ranged from about $35 for a half-hour reading and up to $100 for a full hour.

Lily Dale, New York

Cassadaga's sister community is Lily Dale, New York, sixty miles south of Buffalo. It's larger than Cassadaga and older, established in 1879. The community is better organized than

Cassadaga, with a roster of workshops, lectures, and special events. But the events take place only between June 24 and September 4, when you have to pay a fee to even get into the town. During these months in 2011, for instance, Lily Dale offers daily meditations in its Healing Temple; healing services; a message service (where mediums bring through messages for people in the audience); and a guest speaker and clairvoyant in its auditorium.

Cassadaga has the advantage of good weather, so it's open year round. It does tend to slow down during the summer, but there are always mediums and psychics available for readings. Lily Dale, like Cassadaga, maintains a roster of approved mediums. Homes within the camps in both towns can't be purchased; they can only be leased by mediums in good standing with the association.

These two communities are the only ones of their kind in the United States, so if you're surrounded by skeptics in your life, try one of these places. You might be overwhelmed by how readily everyone—visitors and residents alike—accepts the reality of spirit communication.

How a Medium Works

Mediums have different ways of working with spirits and interpreting the information they receive. The methods are varied and there are no hard and fast rules.

Some mediums use tools to get into their zone. Hazel Burley begins her reading with small, colored pieces of cardboard. The client chooses a certain number of squares and Hazel uses the colors to tune in on the person. Once she's tuned in, she doesn't use the colored squares anymore.

Others don't need any such tools. Vicki de Laurentis, a medium in New York, says that when she gives a reading, whether in a group setting or individually, she takes several deep breaths to calm herself and to clear her mind. She then opens herself to information and messages. Vicki requests that a client ask a specific question, but not give any leading information. Elaboration doesn't help her at all.

One woman who came to Vicki had a simple question about her health and the nausea she was experiencing: would she get better soon? "I quickly keyed in on the fact that the nausea was the result of the chemo she was receiving for breast cancer. She was amazed because she hadn't told anyone about the condition. I told her she would recover and she did. I gave her such a clear reading because she just asked the one simple question."

Spirits often come to Vicki whether she wants them to or not. After 9/11, a father from their community who had died in one of the buildings materialized in the back seat of her car. He wouldn't leave her alone until Vicki went to his wife six months later. "He was very persistent. I think he'd been trying to find someone close to her who could hear him."

There are times, Vicki says, when she just can't get a clear reading on someone. The individual's fear may block information or Vicki herself may be affected by the person. "If it affects my own stuff it can be difficult. I've had to stop readings early just because the person's energy is draining me. Energy vampires are the most difficult for readings. I usually have to end them early because I can't take it. I have literally gotten migraine headaches."

Natalie Thomas, a medium in Australia, begins her preparation before the client arrives, by being rested and hydrated so that she can be "a clear vessel." As the mother of teens and toddlers, being rested isn't always possible. "So I just ask Spirit to give me a bit of a zap." On her way to a reading, she often sings uplifting songs at the top of her lungs in order to lift her vibration. She also meditates the night before. "If I'm feeling shattered, I postpone my readings. I don't feel right about charging for a lousy experience."

Her clients, she says, play a part in how the reading unfolds. Some people walk into the shop and she simply knows she's going to experience a terrific connection. Other times, "It's excruciatingly difficult, almost like wading through mud. This is because of their belief system and the state of their energy field. When that occurs, the readings tend to be less about spirit contact and more about counseling."

Whenever Natalie is confronted with a client who is sad, with dense energy, she teaches them ways to tune in to their own guidance, to navigate their way through emotional turmoil by using meditation, prayer, writing, cleansing of the energy field. When a client is grieving due to the death of a loved one, "then the mediumship is full on, in order to help them heal." Her goal is to bring comfort in whatever way is best on that particular day, for that particular client. She tries to teach others how "to light their own divine spark in order to bring healing to our planet."

Usually, Natalie hears messages through her right ear, as if someone was whispering to her. Sometimes, names are muffled and Natalie ends up with an approximate name. One time she heard the name Missy Pippy. "The client laughed and said it was her granddaughter, whom she addressed as Missy, but her deceased husband called her Popeye. Her name was actually Poppy, and he was trying to tie it all together in my ear to pass his love on to his only granddaughter."

Connie Cannon has been a medium most of her adult life, and over the years, has developed certain parameters and rules that she doesn't violate. She prefers not to have any personal information about the client, other than a first name. "My information comes through disembodied entities. One of my rules is to never give death predictions, under any circumstances. I am, however, a voice for spirit and I've learned to trust their judgment."

So when a middle-aged client from Germany made an appointment to see her one April, Connie had only her first name to go on. The day of Jan's appointment, Connie entered an altered state. Her otherworldly helpers instructed her to tell Jan that she was reaching the light at the end of a long, hard tunnel, that from this point forward her life would improve beyond her wildest imagination. They also told Connie that Jan's husband—who was middle aged and healthy—would sustain a massive stroke in late May, be placed in a full-care nursing home, and that by the end of June he would make his transition to the other side. After that, Jan's burdens would be lifted.

Connie silently argued with her helpers. The prediction, after all, was one of death. But her guides' instructions were clear: *Tell her now.* Connie told Jan exactly what her helpers had said. That night, Jan called Connie and confessed to being locked in a terrible marriage to a brutal husband from whom there was no escape. She had purchased a gun and had planned to kill herself that very afternoon. But after her reading, she felt as if she had a reason to continue, and disposed of the gun.

Connie didn't hear from Jan again until July, when she dropped by Connie's home to give her an update. Jan's husband, John, had sustained a massive, debilitating stroke in May, had been placed in a nursing home, and had died on June 30, just forty-five minutes before the end of June, as Connie's spirit helpers had said. "In this instance, a revelation of the husband's departure was obviously deemed necessary to prevent Jan from killing herself. She'd tolerated all that she could, which Spirit knew and I did not know. Today, Jan owns a small German restaurant, lives in a wonderful retirement community, and has a genuinely happy life."

Mediums are not so different from the rest of us. They have spouses, families, hopes and dreams, disappointments and triumphs. But because they speak to the dead, because the spirits of the dead whisper in their ears, they may provide insights that benefit you, heal you, relieve your grieving and anxiety, and help you move forward with your life.

Knock, Knock, Who's There?

If you're curious about whether there are spirits around you, here's one experiment you and a friend can try.

Pick a spot in your house or outside where you'll meditate for a few minutes. Before you start, take several photos of the area with a digital camera. Chances are, the photos will look exactly like the area does when you see it without the camera. Now settle in for a brief meditation. Do so by requesting that if there are spirits around you, they will manifest themselves in the digital photos that your partner takes.

During your meditation, try to keep your mind empty, your thoughts still. When you initially enter a meditative state, your thoughts may be scurrying around like hungry mice, distracting you from what you're trying to do. Meditate for about ten minutes.

If any spirits manifest themselves, they may do so as orbs or as white or gray wisps that resemble smoke. A skeptic might tell you there's a light leak in the camera, but you'll recognize the difference between orbs, wisps like smoke—and a light leak!

Alternately, look for a special spot in nature that seems energetically charged. Take half a dozen photos. The results may surprise you.

We've gotten into the habit of doing this when we travel. A few years ago, when we visited the rural Virginia home of a prominent remote viewer, or clairvoyant, and his wife, we admired a statue of Buddha they had in their yard. The little Buddha sat beneath a tree, surrounded by flowers and singing birds. The area emanated such peace that we snapped a picture of him. We were astonished to see a ghostly image, like fog or mist, had manifested around the Buddha. We turned the camera toward the nearby forest and took another picture. To our surprise, four tall, wispy figures appeared at the edge of the forest.

Trust the process in any experiment that you try. Request a manifestation. Expect it to happen.

Mediums in Other Cultures

In some cultures, mediumship is not only accepted, mediums are regarded as special individuals who help mitigate disputes, provide advice and counsel during crises, and restore harmony to communities. In Brazil, a belief in spirits and mediums is widespread. In Africa, notably in Mozambique, spirit contact, mediumship, and even spirit possession are prevalent. In Haiti, practitioners of voodoo work themselves into trance states and communicate messages from the spirits that possess them.

In Cuba, the Dominican Republic, Puerto Rico, and Brazil, Santeria is widely practiced. Even though its practice is forbidden in Cuba, it's believed that Castro himself practiced Santeria. Lydia Cabrera, who until her death was the foremost expert in the world on Santeria, contended that Fidel Castro was actually a *mayombero*, a practitioner of the dark side of Santeria, and used this particular brand of witchcraft to maintain his power.

Santeria literally means "the worship of saints," and is a union of ancient African magic and Catholic mysticism. It's also practiced among Cubans who have settled in the United States. Scattered about South Florida are botanicas, little shops that sell the tools of the santero's trade: intricately carved figures of saints, ornate porcelain containers, halves of coconuts, bottles of herbs and perfumes, statues, candles, and cowrie shells and Brisca cards, which are used in divination and to clarify spirit messages.

The origin of Santeria lies in Nigeria, home of the Yoruba people. During the centuries of slave trading, thousands of Yorubas were transported to the New World, and many of those whose journey ended in Latin America and the Caribbean were strongly influenced by the Catholic saints. Over the years, qualities of the Yoruba gods and goddesses were combined with those of particular saints, creating *orishas*. When a santero worships a particular *orisha*, he believes he becomes imbued with supernatural powers. Through magical rituals, he supposedly can cure illnesses, divine the future, and help you to manifest your dreams.

When we met, Trish was teaching English to Cuban refugees who had come to the United States on the *Mariel* boatlift.

Through one of her students, she learned of a Miami santero, Ruben Delgado, who had come over during the boatlift. Although Ruben was usually booked weeks in advance, we experienced three repetitions of the name/word Ruben during a period of just several hours, so we followed this cluster of synchronicities and called Ruben to make an appointment. It turned out he had an opening the next day, so one warm Saturday morning we drove to Ruben's home in Little Havana to watch him work.

He was twenty-seven, a handsome Latino with black hair and liquid dark eyes. He wore a white shirt and loose white cotton pants that he rolled to his knees. He was barefoot. He explained this was how his main spirit guide, Francisco, dressed when he was alive. Francisco was a very old black man with a bad left leg, a slave brought to Cuba from the Congo during the 1800s, who became Ruben's guide when he was in his teens.

We took seats in Ruben's workroom with several clients. It was cluttered with statues of saints, candles that burned on shelves and tables, delicate porcelain plates that held beads of honey, sweets, food, and loose change, all offerings to the *orishas*. Fresh flowers perfumed the air. He sprinkled the room and everyone in it with Florida water, a light cologne used for spiritual cleansing. He puffed on a thick cigar and blew clouds of smoke around his chair. Santeros believe that smoke, like certain types of cologne, releases beneficial energy.

Ruben, seated on a chair in the center of the room, had a blue cloth spread across his lap. He recited the Lord's Prayer, then chanted a spiritual mass. His voice gradually increased in pitch, his breathing quickened, then his body convulsed as if jolted by electrical shocks. Spittle ran from the corners of his mouth, the cigar fell to the floor, his eyes rolled back in their sockets until only the whites showed. Then he began to talk, using words he didn't normally use. He gave predictions for his clients and conducted a ritualized healing for an illness that Francisco said was caused by *brujeria*, witchcraft.

The most fascinating part of this four-hour session was that while in trance, Ruben could apparently defy physical laws. On two occasions, he ground the glowing end of a cigar along his forearm and when the ashes were brushed away, there were no visible burn marks. Ruben also gulped from a bottle of rum, then smashed it on the tile floor and danced barefoot on the broken glass. Like worshippers of the Hindu deity Lord Subramanian, who pierce their bodies with sharp objects during an annual festival, he showed no sign of pain, his feet didn't bleed, and he didn't appear drunk. In his everyday life, Ruben was teetotaler.

MEDIUMS AND DECEASED PETS

For animal lovers, the death of a pet can be as traumatic as the death of a family member. Animals, like humans, often go to great lengths to communicate with the people they have left behind, so don't be surprised if, during a reading with a medium, one of your beloved pets stops by.

During a fundraiser, a woman sat down at Natalie Thomas's table for a reading. Natalie immediately felt a powerful energy around her. A spirit was coming to say that he loved her and to thank her for loving him. The woman asked the person's name, but all Natalie picked up was "Frog." When she asked if this was someone's nickname, her client burst into tears.

It turned out that Frog was a little Staffordshire Terrier, who was quite wild. Friends had given him away because they couldn't care for him. He kept jumping her client's fence, hence the name

Frog. But because he was so small, he kept hurting himself trying to get over the top of the fence. "My client had cared for him and loved him as much as any human could, and in return he was watching over her from the other side. Through me, he sent his love for her. It was a very powerful experience."

Spirits and Halloween

In the United States, Halloween has become a commercial bonanza on a par with Valentine's Day. You carve pumpkins, decorate your yard with scary stuff—cobwebs and ghosts, witches and goblins—and of course, you buy bags of candy to give out to the trick-or-treaters, who arrive at your door in their incredible costumes, with their gleeful hollers of "Trick or treat!"

But the real message of Halloween doesn't have anything to do with costumes and candy. At sunset on October 31, the Samhain, the Celtic New Year, begins and the boundary between the physical world and that of spirit is believed to be at its thinnest. It's a night to honor the spirits of your ancestors, to meditate, to reach out to the spirits of loved ones who have passed on. Express your gratitude to them for having enriched your life. Clear away the psychic debris in your life and make way for the new—new relationships, opportunities, thoughts, and ideas.

If you seek contact with loved ones who have passed on, then Halloween is a favorable time to initiate communication. It's most powerful at midnight. Here are some tips:

- Find your special, quiet spot. If you live in an area where you can sit outside, then do so. Otherwise, do this inside your home, in an spot that is special to you.
- Imagine yourself surrounded in a cocoon of white light.
- Light a candle that represents someone you know who has passed on. Give thanks to the person for the role he or she played in your life. Ask for the individual to contact you in some way.
- Write your desires on a piece of paper. These desires can be anything. If you've got a manuscript you hope to see published, jot that down. If you would like a raise, include that on your list. New job or contract? Include it. Want to hear from your deceased mother or experience more synchronicity in your life? Put all of it on your list.
- Focus on your wish list. Then burn the piece of paper.
- When the embers are cool, blow them into the night sky.

8

CLUSTER BUSTERS

Stand in an enclosed room and scream. Those echoes you hear are similar to the echoes that spirits leave when they try repeatedly to communicate with us. You may be able to hear the echoes of their voices, but even if you can't, you'll recognize other kinds of echoes—repetitions of names, numbers, birthdates, animals, certain foods, smells. Clusters involve repetition—the same three numbers that you see everywhere, for example. Or a name that you encounter over and over. Or a scent or odor that seems to permeate the very air you breathe.

Clusters can also be a series of unrelated events that occur in the same building, room, or location. Electrical equipment acts up, room temperatures change for no apparent reason, doorbells ring on their own, phones ring even though no one is calling, TVs and radios go off and on by themselves, you may hear voices, or catch movement in your peripheral vision. These clusters are similar to hauntings, but with marked differences.

In hauntings, the spirits are often caught in a desperate loop. They may not realize they're dead or their emotional attachments to physical life are so powerful they're unable to move on. Sometimes, hauntings are caused by energy remnants of the people who lived in a building or of events that took place there. Hauntings can be frightening, disturbing.

If spooky, repetitious incidents occur that you can't explain as ordinary events, use your emotions as a gauge. If you're fearful, or sense something dreadful related to the unusual occurrences, then it's probably a haunting rather than a friendly visit from the spirit world.

Words, Names, Numbers

This grouping appears to be the most common type of cluster. While there are no hard and fast rules with spirit contact and clusters, names, numbers, or words are often personally significant. You might be on your way to work, for example, and in the course of an hour see three license plates containing the numbers 612 in that order—startling enough by itself. But suppose the numbers happen to be those of your recently deceased mother's birthday—June 12?

Consider spending some time meditating when you get home. Your mother may be trying to get in touch with you from the other side. The incident could be her way of warning you to exercise caution in some area of your life, or it could be confirming your hope that awareness continues on past death.

Perhaps a friend with an unusual name recently passed away, and suddenly you notice or hear the name everywhere—on the car radio, on TV, in a book. Then one evening while you're at home and cleaning out your attic, you run across a box of old letters you forgot you saved and find several from your deceased friend. This combination of synchronicity and spirit contact is difficult to dismiss as meaningless. But some people do because it's easier or less frightening to stick to the beliefs they have than to embark on a journey into the unknown.

This journey, after all, is not without risk. If your partner or family and friends are firmly entrenched in a belief system that frowns upon psychic or spiritual exploration, then your journey may not sit well with them. Relationships may unravel and fall apart. Many people whose partners are skeptical of this area pursue it on their own, in the shadows, as a separate and private part of their lives. Younger people, high school and college students in particular, may feel alienated at times because their beliefs are so radically different from those of their peers.

Hopefully, your partner, family, and friends are either fellow explorers or, at the very least, supportive of your explorations. In either of those environments, you should be able to embark on your expansive journey without any fear of losing the people and circumstances that ground you.

Words

Sometimes, tragedy is a wakeup call that suddenly triggers our awareness of a deeper order in the universe. We quickly learn that the language of this hidden order is synchronicity and that it's a vehicle through which spirits communicate with us. When that tragedy involves the death of a child, the wakeup call seems particularly onerous and harsh.

In 2007, Bee's daughter, Meghan, was diagnosed with a malignant cancer of the brainstem that primarily targets children between the ages of three and ten. Approximately 150–200 kids each year are diagnosed with it, and the median survival from diagnosis day is nine months. More than 90 percent die within two years of diagnosis. This disease is basically a death sentence for these kids.

Meghan died about nine months after her diagnosis, in July 2008. She was thirteen years old. In early August 2010, within a period of about four hours, the word "phoenix" appeared to Bee seven times. A word cluster. She recognized it. "At the seventh appearance, I started to cry because I felt something elusive was being communicated to me. Phoenix, Arizona, was where Meghan died. In many cultural mythologies, phoenix is the bird that symbolizes rebirth from death. I knew this was not a coincidence."

The next day, she was at her therapist's office and mentioned her experience with the phoenix cluster. He then told her that his dog's name was Phoenix—an eighth incident of the word. Since then, phoenix has appeared to her at least once a day in many forms: Joaquin Phoenix; banner ads for the University of Phoenix; in the form of a movie, *Flight of the Phoenix;* in the form of a newspaper, *Boston Phoenix.*

Interestingly, it won't appear if she purposefully looks for it. One day, Bee actually set out to find the word, but finally gave up. That night, her husband was watching *Seinfeld* on TV and George Costanza said, "Phoenix" just as she was getting into bed. "I said, 'Thank you, Meghan,' and went to sleep with a smile on my face."

In September 2010, Bee ran across *The 7 Secrets of Synchronicity* while she was at Barnes & Noble and paged through it. That same night, she Googled our names and found our synchronicity blog. She began reading the daily posts, but didn't make a comment for several months.

In October 2010, Bee was struck by the drama unfolding at Camp Esperanza, where thirty-three Chilean miners were carried up from the depths of the earth by a capsule named *Phoenix*. Then in early November, we posted commentary about the 2010 election, in which the Republican Party rose, like a phoenix from the ashes, out of its defeat two years earlier and took over the U.S. House of Representatives. We used an image of a phoenix in the post. Shortly after that, the hits to our blog soared. We noticed on our counter, Sitemeter, that the majority of these visitors found the blog by using "phoenix" as their search term.

In late November, we put up another post about phoenix, mentioning the repeated hits with this term from all over the world. We speculated that perhaps the clusters of the word indicated a pattern that was developing in the collective unconscious. And that was the post that prompted Bee to write us and tell us her story. "I would have been happy to remain a silent reader, but your *Phoenix* entry electrified me," said Bee.

Names
Synchronistic name clusters that point to spirit contact are often eerily literal. The name, for example, may be that of the spirit who seeks to communicate with you. Or it could be a relative of the spirit. Whenever you start seeing or hearing repetition of a name, be sure to note it in your synchronicity journal—with the date, time, circumstances.

Since we are such mobile people, it isn't surprising that many clusters occur while we're traveling. Whether you're in a car, train, or plane, clusters are out there, if you're open and receptive to them.

Natalie Thomas often encounters synchronicity in her work. So when she was out driving one day, she knew something important was happening when she passed six cars with the name Jen on the license plates.

Since Natalie also has a friend named Jen, the cluster really caught her attention. However, as far as Natalie knew, Jen wasn't facing any crisis, wasn't in any sort of trouble. She thought no more about it. The next morning, Jen called Natalie to tell her she'd just found her mother dead in her home.

As Natalie rushed over to Jen's house, a car pulled up alongside her with a license plate that had the name Jac on it. Jen's mother's name was Jacqui. "I immediately 'saw' Jacqui dancing and swirling in a vortex with her husband, Les, who had passed on some time ago."

In this experience, the Jen cluster proved to be precognitive. The astonishing synchronicity of the Jac license plate near Jacqui's house seemed to be the exclamation point at the end of it. Out of all the names in the universe, why that particular name at that particular time?

It's as if the universe is choreographing events and creating a fertile environment in which these seamless synchronicities can occur.

Numbers

Synchronicity loves numbers as much or more than it does names. And why not? We're surrounded by numbers—license plates, bank accounts, driver's licenses, Social Security numbers, birthdates, phone and cell numbers, TV stations, even our ranking within a family, such as the third child. Numbers possess a certain purity, an unequivocal power that can't be denied, argued with, annihilated. Carl Jung considered numbers to be archetypes. He said that when you experience a cluster of the same number or numbers, it means that archetype has become active within your psyche. And if it's active within you, then it can be more easily used by those in spirit who hope to communicate with you.

Of course, not every cluster of numbers is spirit contact. Some are synchronicities that act as confirmations, warnings, guidance, and signal a shift in your personal consciousness. Other number synchronicities might signal a shift in our collective consciousness as a species, as inhabitants of the same planet. One such cluster is 11:11, or a variation, like 11 or 1:11.

Since we wrote about 11:11 in *The 7 Secrets of Synchronicity*, the awareness of this sequence of numbers has long since reached a tipping point. If you Google "11:11," several hundred million links come up. Perhaps it means that some sort of mass paradigm shift is underway in the world.

On a personal level, if you're one of those individuals who sees 11:11 everywhere—on your microwave, your bedside clock, your cell phone, the timer on the treadmill at your gym—then you may be more open not only to recognizing synchronicity, but to spirit contact. So don't be surprised if a deceased loved one uses these numbers in some way to communicate with you.

If 11:11 is, as many people believe, related to a higher dimension of consciousness, then the communication with spirit could take a variety of forms. You might start glimpsing ghostly figures, hearing noises that have no apparent cause, smelling fragrances that remind you of your mom, dad, sister, spouse, or friend. Keep notes, just as you would with any synchronicity. Be specific about the time of day, what you were thinking about before you noticed the numbers or experienced ghostly presences. Include details about what you felt at the moment it was happening. In retrospect, such details are usually difficult to recall.

Some people become obsessed by repetitive numbers, whether it's 11:11, 12:12, 3:33, 10:10, or others. They might proclaim these numbers are initiated by spirit guardians or celestial beings, who seek to seize our attention so they can help "lift us to a higher vibration." Some of these true believers might be quite sincere. Others might hope to sell you a book, CD, or DVD containing "secret" knowledge. You might be asked to join a group or e-mail list or subscribe to a site so that you, too, can be among the special few who will rise to a "new vibration" or be protected from coming disasters. Such offers are often scams or the work of a would-be cult leader looking for followers and money.

While websites, blogs, and books are all great resources, you are the ultimate authority in your own life and only you can determine if a cluster is personally significant.

One woman wrote that when she experiences "clock clusters" of 11:11, 4:44, 5:55, or any other combination that might appear on a clock, she knows she's in for a rough time. "These number sequences, and particularly 11:11 are an indicator that I am undergoing a karmic lesson." She hasn't taken anyone else's word for it; she has learned through personal experience.

When you're clueless about what a cluster might mean, don't dismiss it as meaningless. If the cluster caught your attention to begin with, then take note of it. Record the details of the experience, your location at the time, the weather, what you were thinking about and feeling, anything that may be pertinent. This way, if the cluster reappears later, you'll have a record of it.

YOUR CLUSTERS

Once you become aware of clusters, you'll discover that they occur more frequently, and for a while, you may be inundated by such experiences. You may find that you have a natural affinity for certain types of clusters and that spirits use this cluster for communicating with you. As a pattern develops, be sure to keep detailed notes. Over time, it's likely that other patterns will unfold. You might, for instance, relate a particular number cluster to your deceased father or to a friend who passed on or a frequent name cluster could be the vehicle your grandmother uses to communicate with you.

Don't discount any kind of cluster, regardless of how strange or alien it seems to your usual way of thinking. Even food clusters can be vehicles for spirit communication!

Clusters of Foods

This is one of the strangest types of clusters we've run across. But if spirits use anything at their disposal for contact, why should foods be exempt?

The MO for this one starts from a premise: there's a particular food that you associate with a really great period of your life and/ or with a loved one who has passed on. The type of food is irrelevant. But when you suddenly encounter it repeatedly—through conversations, in restaurants, books, dreams, on websites—then you're definitely experiencing a food cluster and better take a deeper look.

Over the July Fourth weekend in 2010, Jenean, an artist and writer then living in Delaware, was in her kitchen, about to make a brunch for herself and her grandson. She asked if he would like to sample some of the new birthday fig preserves her sister, Heather, had given her. Jenean remarked how much she loved these preserves, that they simply aren't available in Delaware. She marveled at how strange it was that Heather had found fig preserves at a T.J. Maxx in Dover, Delaware, that had been grown and preserved in Rogers, Arkansas, of all places.

"Rogers is a little town in between Bentonville and Springdale, an area where many of our ancestors settled, where there is still family land and where my brother lived at the time of his death, so it holds special significance for me," says Jenean.

While in the midst of their discussion about figs, there was a knock at the carport door. The next-door neighbor had dropped by to tell them she was just at a little farmers' market up the road and saw fresh figs there.

Figs. Again. Two mentions within minutes of each other. Jenean says it had been at least two years since she had mentioned figs to this neighbor. Yet here the neighbor was, talking about figs. That night, Jenean clicked into the counter gadget on her blog that provides information about the visitors, including their location. She saw that someone from Rogers, Arkansas, had just visited her blog for the first time.

Jenean's brother died in 1991, under mysterious circumstances. Some of her fondest memories were from her childhood, when she and her brother spent hours picking and eating figs. "I can still remember the sticky feel of the leaves and the figs and the heat of the summer when we picked them." She felt this was actual contact with her brother's spirit. "His only child is grown now and has children of her own and has been talking to me for a couple of weeks about her father's death and burial. So perhaps all of this is intertwined somehow."

Many of these synchronicity clusters and spirit contact seem to take place in a kind of twilight zone that even Rod Serling might find perplexing. In a sense, you have to become a detective, as Bee did when she began encountering the word "phoenix," make your connections, then surrender to the mystery of it all. The exploration is part of the magic of this journey; how each step, each twist and turn, leads you into an even deeper mystery, another layer of synchronicity and spirit contact.

After two years, our blog on synchronicity, *www.synchrosecrets .com/synchrosecrets,* has accumulated more than a thousand posts that cover every conceivable type of meaningful coincidence you might experience. Even if each post has only twenty comments, that's 20,000 comments from people in all walks of life, from more than 175 countries, from various religious and cultural backgrounds. Many of the comments offer personal stories about synchronicity, spirit contact, and the emotional and spiritual evolution people experience in their daily lives. A significant percentage of these anecdotes involve clusters.

Clusters seize our attention. The repetition of names, numbers, phrases, words, animals, whatever it is, tends to drive home the fact that something unusual is happening, that you should pay attention. Clusters are one way the universe speaks to you intimately, one on one, about an issue that may be holding you back or about an idea or belief that may move you forward.

Change is a constant in our lives. If we resist it, we flounder, we suffer. If we go with it, our lives are enriched in unimagined ways. Synchronicity occurs when the inner stuff that makes us who we are manifests itself in the outer world and the two become one. Synchronicity.

The Spirit of Places

Have you ever felt drawn to a particular location? It might be a village or city, a certain country, or even an ancient landmark of some kind. You feel so drawn to this location that you dream about it, read everything you can find about it, talk about it and, finally, you plan a trip to this area. All along, it's as if the ancestral spirit of this place has been speaking to you and that voice has awakened something inside of you.

This type of spirit contact is radically different from the kinds of contact we've been talking about. During this type of contact, we may actually be tapping into the collective soul or spirit of a place—the confluence of emotions, spirituality, and thoughts of the people who inhabited it. Such was the case for two women from different backgrounds who felt they were called to an ancient stone forest in the Peruvian Andes, known as Markawasi. We had never heard of this unusual place where many people have reported spirit and UFO contact until we met Kathy Doore of West Palm Beach.

Markawasi sits at 12,800 feet above sea level, on a plateau that is about 3 miles long and a mile wide. This plateau contains hundreds of giant stone figures, but no one knows how old they are, who made them, or whether they were sculpted over the centuries by the wind and the elements. Many of the statues resemble animals that aren't indigenous to the Andes—tortoises, elephants, sea lions, frogs. There are faces and figures that resemble other cultures—the African queen, a sphinx, a pharaoh, Nefertiti, and other Egyptian deities. These massive stones are eerily similar to those on Easter Island and some of them bear an uncanny resemblance to stone remnants found at other sacred sites worldwide.

In *Markawasi: Peru's Inexplicable Stone Forest*, author Kathy Doore writes, "With its mysterious and stunning monuments emulating Egyptian deities . . . and its claims of spontaneous healings, plus recorded testimony of ultra-dimensional visitors, the mysterious plateau is believed to be the remnant of a proto-historical culture previous to the Great Flood." We learned from Kathy that it took her twenty-five years to get to Markaswasi, a place to which she felt called, and when she did arrive, it changed her life.

Lydia Colon, a bilingual interpreter and artist, was "called" to Markawasi in 1999, while sitting in bed and enjoying the sunrise over Cuzco, Peru, where she lived at the time. "I had a vision of a huge stone spelling out the word 'Markawasi' and heard a resonant, god-like voice say, 'Markawasi.' I knew the vision was a call and that I must go," she told Doore, who included the story in her book.

Colon and Doore met around the same time that Colon first went to Markawasi, while Doore was on a pilgrimage to Machu Picchu. Colon believes "the spirits themselves had brought us together."

If you feel called to such a location, as these two women did, then you will undoubtedly experience clusters related to that place. Don't dismiss them as meaningless. Follow them, see where they lead you. Once you heed that call, it's likely you'll experience a higher coordinating force. Synchronicity will be your traveling companion and your contact with spirit is apt to be profound and life changing.

Layered Synchronicities and Spirit Contact

In *The 7 Secrets of Synchronicity*, we wrote about an empath and friend, Renie Wiley, who occasionally worked with police, using her empathic abilities to provide information on unsolved cases. We accompanied her to a police station in late 1984 to work on a missing child case.

On May 24, 1984, eight-year-old Christie Luna had walked to a store near her home in Green Acres, Florida, to buy some cat food and never returned. The police suspected foul play, and Renie confirmed as much when she used Christie's stuffed toys to tune in on the girl. As an empath, she felt what Christie felt when her mother's boyfriend used to beat her and reported the girl was deaf in one ear because of the beatings. Christie's mother later confirmed this fact.

Later that night, we left the station with Renie and one of the police officers and drove around, following Renie's directions until we arrived at a wooded area surrounded by a high barbed-wire fence. Renie felt that Christie's body was buried somewhere in the woods. In spite of a search, the body was not found.

Skip ahead twenty-four years to 2008. Psychic Dennie Gooding called to tell us she would be visiting our area in March and that she would be working on a missing person case. We agreed to a get-together and invited several others to join us.

The day before the festivities, we were going through some old books, weeding out what we no longer needed. A check fell out of one of the books. It was dated 1986, made out to us for $50, repayment on a loan, and was signed Renie Wiley. Renie had passed away in the early 1990s, and we were astonished the check had been inside the book all these years. We wondered if

Renie was trying to contact us and we just hadn't been aware of it. In all the years since she had passed away, we'd never experienced any contact with her.

The night of the gathering at our house, Dennie told us she'd been hired by a police officer at the Palm Beach County sheriff's department who worked in the cold cases division. When she began describing the case, Trish suddenly interrupted her. "Is this the Christie Luna case?"

Dennie's eyes widened with shock. "Yes. But how did you know?"

"You're not going to believe this," Rob said, and walked over to the drawer where we'd put Renie's check, and brought it out. "Here's how we know." Then we told her the story.

It was as if Renie had reached out from the afterlife through the unsolved disappearance of Christie Luna, and the psychic who had been hired to delve into it nearly a quarter of a century later. The synchronicities were remarkably layered and the contact occurred in an unusual way. Here are the facts:

- Renie and Dennie never met. Renie died several years before we met Dennie through a Canadian astrologer who touted her psychic ability and gave us her contact information. If Trish hadn't left a comment on his blog about his post on Mercury's retrograde during the 2000 presidential election, they probably wouldn't have communicated at all and we never would have met Dennie.
- Rob had a reading with Dennie in 2002. Afterward, we gave her name to another friend, Nancy, who recommended Dennie to the wife of the police officer who eventually hired her to delve into the Christie Luna case.
- Dennie identified the same wooded area that Renie did as the place where Christie's remains would be found.

- Neither of us remember sticking Renie's check inside a book. In fact, in 1986, we were just starting out as writers, money was tight, and it's likely we would have cashed the check as soon as we'd gotten it.

The clusters here involved Christie Luna and the two psychics who, separated by nearly twenty-five years, worked on the case. What about the spirit contact? Was it Christie's spirit that led Renie to the fenced wooded area? Was it Renie's spirit that led Dennie to the same area a quarter of a century later? Was our finding the check from Renie her way of communicating with us?

At any point in the past, different decisions might have been made and none of the events described here would have happened. So who was orchestrating all this, anyway? And that's always the bottom line, isn't it?

Christie's body has never been found and the case remains open. Just within the last year, an article appeared in the *Palm Beach Post* about the unsolved murder. It's possible that at some point in the future, another psychic will tackle this case and the mystery about Christie Luna will be resolved.

A religious individual might see the hand of a divine being in synchronicity and spirit contact. An atheist might just shrug all of it off to random weirdness. But if everything and everyone is connected at some level, then perhaps the quantum physicists have the best answer. "It will be ultimately misleading and indeed wrong to suppose . . . that each human being is an independent actuality who interacts with other humans beings and with nature," writes David Bohm in *Wholeness and the Implicate Order*. "In the implicate order, we have to say that mind enfolds matter in general and therefore the body in particular. Similarly, the body enfolds not only the mind but also in some sense the entire material universe."

Not every experience you have with spirit contact and clusters will be as complex or layered as this one. Most of them tend to be fairly straightforward—once you realize what's actually going on. If you feel emotionally elevated with the contact, then by all means proceed—and surrender to the experience.

9

OBJECTS OF
INTEREST

Spirits often use objects in various way to communicate
with us. We've compiled a list of some of the most common experiences involving objects. You can't always attribute spirit contact to these experiences, but it's worth
considering as a possibility, depending on your circumstances. Check the ones that apply to you:

❑ I've heard rapping sounds that have no apparent cause.

❑ Sometimes lights, TVs, radios, or CD players turn on by themselves.

❑ I've seen reflections in mirrors and windows of faces or objects that aren't physically present.

❑ I've seen initials or names that appear on steamed or frosted glass windows.

❑ Objects sometimes mysteriously disappear then reappear in other locations.

❑ A car or an appliance wouldn't start, but later it worked fine and there was nothing wrong with it.

❑ Objects, such as books, figurines, or plates have inexplicably toppled off shelves or counters.

❑ Objects have appeared where they don't belong, and they seem to address a question I've had about someone who has passed on.

❑ I've heard voices, murmurings, or music that has no apparent cause or source.

❑ I've found the same object repeatedly where it simply wasn't possible for it to be.

❑ I've noted the sudden appearance of a type of bird or other animal that is rarely, if ever, seen where I live.

❑ I've had repeated visitations by the same wild animal.

❑ I've experienced strong sensations that I'm not alone at times when I've been home by myself.

❑ I've walked into a room and felt an unseen presence.

❑ Sometimes my pet acts as if someone else is nearby when I'm the only one here.

❑ I've experienced a sense of being protected by unseen forces.

❑ I've found an object that belonged to or was important to a deceased loved one.

❑ I've noticed scents or odors in my environment that have no apparent source or cause.

The Woo-Woo Factor

When you read the list above, how did you react? Some people might immediately associate many of the items as characteristics of mental meltdown, disassociation from reality, delusion. Others who read the same list might feel gratified or relieved as they recognize some of their personal experiences, and acknowledge that others have had similar experiences. And still others might think that most of the examples on the list probably have logical explanations.

For example, lights going off and on could be an electrical brownout. A missing object that shows up in an unexpected place could've gotten there by ordinary means. That said, the items listed are also some of the more common ways that spirits attempt contact with the living. Most people who have experienced contact with spirits probably are familiar with some items in the list.

The next time you're up against a skeptic who rolls her eyes about your spirit contact experiences, there are ways to counteract the negativity:

- If the person prides herself on facts and figures, be sure you have your facts and figures at your fingertips. Never hesitate to gently educate a skeptic. Many times, skeptics are just afraid of what is unfamiliar.
- Don't doubt the validity of your own experiences. If the skeptics in your life exist within your own family or social circles, use your personal experiences and stories as proof.

Even for a skeptic, it's tough to discount the experiences of someone you love.

- Be clear about who you are and what you believe. When you lack clarity in this area, others pick up on it.
- Believe. If your experiences contradict the teachings of your culture, religion, family, or schools, it doesn't matter as long as you are convinced that your experiences are real.
- Walk away. There are times when this is your only option, when debate and argument simply aren't worth pursuing.
- Transformation. While some friends may fade from your life, you'll attract others with similar beliefs and experiences. You and your new friends will recognize common patterns, learn, and grow.

A Classic Story of Spirit Contact

Shortly before Christmas 1989, Karen A's husband, who owned a restaurant, was killed by a drunk driver. On the night it happened, she and her three children were waiting for him to arrive home. At around 8:30 p.m., they heard "a tremendous boom on the front door, almost as if a gust of wind had hit it," but there was no wind that night. Karen knew something had happened to Rick before the police arrived with the news.

Over the course of the next month, she and her children began to experience classic examples of spirit communication through objects, voices, and electronics:

- They saw their dad's reflection in the windows from inside the house.
- Her eight-year-old daughter reported seeing her dad getting into bed with Karen's youngest child. She said she knew it

was her dad by the chain and medal hanging around his neck.

- Karen and her kids all started hearing their names in loud whispers at close range.
- The TV turned itself on frequently. Karen wishes she had paid more attention to what was on the screen. She thinks she may have missed a message.
- Karen's bedroom light turned on frequently by itself.
- They all heard heavy footsteps on what seemed like the roof. The footsteps sounded as if they were running across the entire length of the house.
- They started seeing the ghostly presence of a man sitting on the toilet upstairs, in the hallway, across from the kitchen.
- One night, Karen was using the upstairs bathroom. The door was open and the house was dark. On the wall in the hall, she saw the shadow of a person walking by.

After this last experience, Karen felt it was best for her family to move into a different home. Their old home sat on the market for a year after they moved out. During this time, Karen allowed a family in need to stay at the house—but never told them about what she and her children had experienced. On the day they moved, they asked if she had been coming in when they weren't at home. She hadn't and asked why they thought that. While cleaning the hallway bathroom, they had closed the door to keep the stink of cleaning solutions from escaping. They had gone out to eat and on their return, the bathroom door was open. They also had heard noises from the attic above the foyer. They thought it might be critters in the attic, but the husband went up to check and didn't find anything.

After the family returned the house keys to her, Karen drove halfway down the block when her car went into neutral while still engaged in drive. She kept pressing the accelerator, but nothing happened. She thought it was her transmission and had the car towed. The dealer couldn't find anything wrong with the car. "In hindsight, I think it may have been my husband urging me to stay in the old house. Given the economy today, he would have been right."

This story bears the signature of contact through objects: TV, lights, reflections in windows, a car that won't move even though nothing is wrong with it. So if this is spirit communication, how can the dead influence matter?

Theories of Spirit Contact

Spiritualists, scientists, and other experts have developed different theories regarding how and why spirits move matter.

Psychokinesis

Psychokinesis is the ability to affect objects with your mind.

When you mention psychokinesis or telekinesis and combine it with Uri Geller, most people immediately associate it with spoon bending, which put Geller on the psychic map. But when the inexplicable movement of objects is linked to after-death communication then, in theory, we're dealing with effects created by the mind or consciousness of the deceased. Such events are jarring and seize our attention. Karen certainly noticed, and over the course of time, the events changed her perspective on the afterlife.

Spirit psychokinesis isn't limited to knockings, voices, or electronics that go off and on by themselves. The phenomenon manifests in numerous ways—initials or names inscribed on steamy or frosty glass; objects that fall off shelves; glass that shatters for no reason; objects found where they shouldn't be or that disappear and reappear. The challenge, of course, is to determine when such incidents have normal explanations and which ones are examples of contact with the other side.

From the Inside Out

Emanuel Swedenborg, the renowned eighteenth-century Swedish scientist, philosopher, and mystic, contended that the afterlife was the primary reality and that physical reality flowed from it; in other words, the physical reality unfolds from the inner reality. This belief preceded the findings of physicist David Bohm.

According to Bohm, the implicate or enfolded order is the deeper reality, a primal soup that births everything in the universe. He referred to our external reality as the explicate order. Interestingly, these ideas echo the accumulated research on near-death experiences and beliefs in most shamanic traditions, where excursions into the afterlife through trance and out-of-body travel are nearly daily occurrences.

While most religions teach that the soul continues in some form after death, science tends to be skeptical because these teachings are based on faith and soul survival can't be proven in a lab, with empirical evidence. Science tends to discount anecdotal evidence as well. As a result, many of us who experience spirit communication, in any form, are predisposed to dismiss it as nonsense, a random quirk, meaningless. We're encouraged to distrust our own experiences and perceptions.

Synchronicity in and of itself is more difficult for science to dismiss. Even skeptics experience meaningful coincidence, but they may not try to connect any dots or decipher the message. Such a mechanistic view of the universe and of life and death discounts any sort of mystery. In this worldview, magical thinking—the willingness to consider meaning in events that take place outside the confines of cause and effect—is considered the realm of deluded, fragmented individuals.

This worldview, this paradigm, is in its death throes. You can hear its choked gasps on skeptic forums, in academic and scientific circles, in the news, in conversations you overhear at the gym, in the grocery store, at work. It's happening in politics, in totalitarian regimes, in nearly every facet of our lives. The status quo simply doesn't work anymore

An underlying shift is under way in nearly every facet of our lives. Too many people are experiencing this kind of phenomena and are seeking answers. When we, as a society, a culture, start asking the same questions, a momentum builds, a tipping point is reached, and a new paradigm is born.

Through Glass and Mirrors

After Mike Perry's daughter died unexpectedly, he and his wife said their goodbyes at the funeral parlor and drove home. His wife went into the kitchen to make tea, and an image appeared on the window—of their daughter, exactly as she had looked when they had last seen her.

"It wasn't a lasting image," Mike noted. "Before I went in to look, it had disappeared."

In some cases, the images created on mirrors and windows, purportedly by spirits to communicate their presence, are seen by large numbers of people.

When Jenean Gilstrap was about twelve, she lived in Winnfield, Louisiana, across the street from her paternal grandmother. One day all the ladies in the family were gathered around, discussing a woman in the community who had died. The woman's family had planned a wake in her home, where she had passed away in her own bed. But shortly after she died, an image in full color appeared in her bureau mirror, an exact image of her as she lay on her deathbed.

The family was understandably concerned about whether the wake should be at the woman's house. But soon it was viewed as a miracle.

"I was somehow allowed to attend the wake," Jenean said. "The casket was set up in the living room and we were allowed to see the mirror in the woman's bedroom, a big round mirror in a wooden frame. In the center of the mirror was the image of the woman in full color." Some people went up to the mirror and tried to rub the image away, but it remained in place. "It was the talk of the town for a long time afterward. I don't remember ever hearing that the image had faded. But it certainly hasn't faded in my memory."

So what purpose did this communication serve? The woman's family was comforted by the image, but the townspeople were suddenly confronted with a miracle, with a kind of magic, an experience none of them would ever forget. And perhaps the experience changed their ideas about what is possible.

Part of the reason glass or mirrors are favored objects for spirit communication is due to the archetypal use of glass and other reflective surfaces—water, stones, crystal balls—in folklore, movies, books, and in some esoteric traditions.

In J. R. R. Tolkien's *Lord of the Rings* trilogy, for instance, the palantir is a spherical stone similar to a crystal ball that enhances clairvoyance and enables telepathy. It allows the person using it to see over great distance and to gather information.

In Persian mythology, the cup of Jamshid was said to be filled with the elixir of immortality and was used for scrying.

In the sixteenth century, Queen Elizabeth was intrigued with an Aztec mirror owned by a man named John Dee. It was said that by gazing into the mirror while in a receptive state of mind, you would have visions. And sometimes, the visions were of the recently departed. The queen believed she saw the spirit of a dead friend while gazing into Dee's mirror.

Among the ancient Greeks, it was believed the dead could not only communicate with the living, but that the living could reach out to the dead. They constructed places called psychomanteums, where priests organized encounters between the living and the dead.

During his travels, Dr. Raymond Moody, best known for his classic book on near-death experiences, *Life After Life,* visited the ruins of such a place on the River Acherton. He later constructed a chamber in his own home, using the same techniques the Greeks used. It's called the Dr. John Dee Memorial Theater of the Mind, after the John Dee who owned the Aztec mirror, and people come and use the chamber to visit with their departed loved ones.

Moody, in an online conversation with Sharon Barbell (*www.psychomanteum.com*), said that he initially felt maybe one in ten people who visited the chamber would have an experience. But so far, 50 percent of the individuals who have visited have experienced something. "The big surprise is that the apparitions actually come out of the mirror . . . the fact that the apparitions talk and you actually hear them is absolutely mind-bending to me."

The Magic Mirror: Scrying

Scrying is the use of a mirror, crystals, or a bowl of water or any other reflective surface to divine the future. If you'd like to try your hand at scrying to initiate spirit contact, here are some tips to do it safely and effectively:

- Don't be frivolous. This tip should be obvious. Scrying isn't something you do while people are hanging out, at a dinner party, drinking. It's not a conversation piece.
- If you feel more comfortable initially trying to see future events rather than attempting contact with the deceased, then start there. Eventually, you can work your way into spirit communication. At the beginning, the point is to become comfortable with whatever tool you're using.
- Any number of tools will work. A bowl of water, a mirror, a piece of crystal: reflective surfaces are best. But a piece of black, shiny obsidian can serve the same function. Experiment with different stones and other tools.
- Before you begin, perform some sort of protective ritual. Say a prayer, visualize white light around yourself, ask that your contact involve only those spirits whose intentions are good. This ritual really isn't about superstitious mumbo jumbo. Whenever you're attempting to communicate with the deceased, through any tool, it's smart to enter into the experiment with protection so that contact is with only positive spirits.

- Keep a pen and paper handy. When you scry, you're entering an altered state, just as you do when you dream. Your impressions are fleeting, quickly forgotten. Record them as soon as you finish.
- Pay attention to synchronicities that occur before, during, and after scrying. The synchronicities are apt to be powerful, their messages direct, unambiguous. Record them immediately.
- Spirit contact through scrying sometimes provides glimpses into the future. Rather than trying to interpret what you're seeing as you're seeing it, just record your impressions, as you would when you awaken from a dream. Then be alert for occurrences, people, names, and cluster synchronicities that are similar to what you experienced when you scryed.

Spirit Contact Through Other Objects

Besides glass and other shiny surfaces, additional common objects for spirit communication are: books; feathers; televisions, radios, phones, appliances, or other electronic devices; billboards; license plates; movies; lights; and food. In other words, virtually any object in the physical world can be used for communication.

A sequence of synchronicities involving food could be a message from your grandfather. White feathers that consistently appear after a visit to your daughter's grave could be contact from her. A book that slips off a shelf and falls open to a passage that reminds you of your mother could be a message from her. Or you may be thinking about an issue that concerns you and whatever you see or hear confirms that a loved one is giving you the answer or insight you need. This kind of synchronicity invariably seizes your attention.

When Janice Cutbush, a retired teacher, found herself caring more frequently for her ninety-two-year-old mother, she began to feel overwhelmed. She had promised her dad that she would always take care of her mother, but the promise was becoming increasingly more difficult to keep. Her mother suffered moderate memory and cognitive impairment and Janice wondered how she could make her efforts less of a job. What would her father want her to do? She got her answer while driving home from a visit with her daughter.

She had stopped for coffee and the man in front of her was buying a Sky Bar, a chocolate bar with four different flavors inside. Her dead father used to love this candy and was always singing the jingle for it: *Sky Bars, it's the four-in-one bar. . . .* Janice hadn't eaten a Sky Bar in years or thought about him singing that jingle, so she bought one, too. Back in the car, as she bit into it, she remembered how her dad always made everything fun, even the worst chores. "I was thinking about all this as a car drove past me with the license plate that read: CK JOY. Seek joy! I knew he was giving me a message that even though it's stressful right now, I need to let more joy into my life."

The synchronicity involved in Janice's experience is layered. She was thinking about her dad and the situation with her mother, wondering how she could keep her promise to him, and then saw a man buying a Sky Bar, a candy she hadn't seen in years, that she associated with her dad. And right afterward, she saw the license plate. All of this happened within the space of a few minutes, and was part of a thought process that had been set in motion during her drive.

This kind of immediate response to a concern or question you have illustrates how the law of attraction works in conjunction with synchronicity. What you see depends on what you're focused on.

So the next time you are deeply in need of an answer about a deceased loved one—or anything else—focus your attention on that question or need, then release it and let the universe, Spirit, and synchronicity help bring it about, possibly using an object as a vehicle for communicating.

SPONTANEOUS CONTACT

Sometimes, spirit communication with a loved one happens on its own, without any request from you, without any conscious attempt at contact. These experiences, which often involve synchronicity, are usually so powerful that you instantly understand what has happened.

Some years ago, Lauren, an artist who lives in New Mexico, was en route to an art residency in Connecticut and stopped at a rest area to have lunch. After she'd finished eating, she spotted a fancy pair of pliers on the ground next to her table. They looked expensive, so she picked them up, tossed them in her car, and drove on.

During her trip, she had an impulse to visit her grandmother's grave in the little town of DeWitt, Nebraska. She hadn't been there since she was a child and didn't even know if it existed anymore. Not only did she find the town on the map, she located the graveyard and planted a black-eyed Susan on her grandmother's grave. She learned that DeWitt's pride was its tool and die factory, founded in the 1920s. The town even had a Vise-Grip "museum."

"When I got to Connecticut and unloaded my car, I found the pliers on the floor. I had forgotten about them. Sure enough, written across the side were the words, *Vise-Grip The Original.* So now, my magic pliers sit on my bureau. In my mind, they're a gift from Grandma."

Lauren could have eaten lunch at any rest stop between New Mexico and Nebraska, but she just happened to choose the one where a pair of Vise-Grip pliers lay on the ground next to her picnic table. She followed an impulse to visit her grandmother's grave, which turned out to be in the very town where Vise-Grip pliers were made. At any point along this path, Lauren could have made a different decision and neither the synchronicity nor the spirit communication would have occurred. And she wouldn't be the owner of a pair of original Vise-Grips!

Mysterious Straight Pins

During Trish's last year in college, she lived in a small apartment on the third floor of an old building in Utica, New York. She and her roommate, Linda, who later became a family court judge in upstate New York, shared their cramped living space with a tabby cat. Early in the school year, Linda's grandmother passed away.

One day not long afterward, Linda's mother found a straight pin on her mother's tombstone. A few days later, Trish and Linda found straight pins scattered around the living room: a pin stuck in a couch cushion, pins lying on the rug, a couple more straight pins on the kitchen table. This began to happen consistently. When Linda mentioned it to her mother, she laughed and said it was Linda's grandmother. "Nana G loved to sew. I've been finding straight pins all over the house, even underlining passages in the Bible."

One weekend when they visited Linda's parents, her mother showed them the straight pins underlining passages in the Bible. The unusual marking had appeared in the aftermath of Nana G's death.

The straight-pin phenomenon continued consistently for several months then gradually stopped. About ten years later, Trish was visiting St. Augustine with Linda and her mother. They were in the Castillo de San Marcos, a tourist landmark and historical site that dates from the seventeenth century. Their footsteps echoed within the empty hallways. The whisper of the past was everywhere, but everything was bare: the thick walls, the well-worn floors, not even a piece of trash in sight.

So the three of them were moving through the interior, marveling at how cool it was despite the summer heat outside. Trish happened to look down and stopped, incredulous, staring at a single straight pin. She picked it up and showed it to Linda's mother. "What're the odds of finding a straight pin in this place?" she asked.

Linda's mother smiled. "I've been feeling Nana G around."

"Looks like she wanted to tour the place with us," Linda remarked.

By accepting that the soul survives, that spirit communication happens through synchronicity, through objects, and other means, you're increasing the chances that it will happen to you.

10

SPIRIT OF THE TRICKSTER

In mythology, the trickster is an archetypal figure often associated with the transition from life to death. Irony and dark humor, shock and surprise are its calling cards. Just ask writer Sharlie West, who is convinced that her home is haunted.

"I've gotten used to the spirits; they were more active when the house was filled with children. One Thanksgiving the family was sitting around the table talking about our occasional spirit visitors. We were drinking wine and gave a Thanksgiving toast, raising our glasses high. My mom said, 'If there are any ghosts, let them make themselves known.' We were all smiling until her wine glass shattered midair into tiny pieces and splattered all over the table. Dead silence after that. I got chills realizing that although we kidded about the spirits, they were definitely there."

You can look at this startling experience as synchronicity or as cause and effect with the effect coming from a disembodied source. Take your choice! Either way, it exemplifies how the trickster works.

In Chapter 1, we related a story about our stay at a hotel in the Dominican Republic that was built around a graveyard. That experience could be interpreted as a trickster encounter. We had moved from the main building where our balcony overlooked the graveyard to a separate building where our porch looked out to the ocean, but it was in that second building on our last night where we experienced a ghostly encounter that sounded like a wrecking ball striking the building. It was as if the spirits were jokingly telling us, "Oh, you thought that other room was too close to the graveyard? Well, guess what? We're over here, too." In fact, we'd belatedly realized that our door to the room was actually closer to the graveyard than the porch we'd abandoned.

Archetypes bubble up from the collective unconscious, a repository of themes and experiences common to all people. Among other archetypes are the hero, the wise old man or woman, the devil, the child, the great mother. They're found in folklore, mythology, legends, fairy tales, dreams, and in divination systems, such as the tarot and astrology. The trickster is often portrayed in legends as a fox, raven, rabbit, or coyote who tricks us by refusing to play by the rules. In mythology, the trickster, such as Loki or Hermes, plays among the gods and through his cunning and trickery becomes a god.

The trickster in mythology is neither good nor evil, but represents the unpredictability of life, the ability to surprise and confound and confuse. He's a rebel who refuses to conform. In spreading strife and deceiving us, the clever trickster redirects our attention, urging us to move in a new direction. The trickster is loyal to no one, manipulates circumstances, bends the rules, and, in doing so, pushes us to change.

THE TRICKSTER'S TRAP

An ancient legend of the Yoruba people of Nigeria tells the story of the deity Eshu. He wore a tall hat that was red on one side and white on the other. He walked between friends, one who saw a red hat, the other who saw a white hat. Later, the men got into an argument about the color of the hat. Each one was convinced that his version was true and that it was obvious. The two friends came to blows, and that's when Eshu walked over. Laughing at the bloodied and angry men, he showed them his two-tone hat.

The hat trick was a way of getting people to understand that sometimes there can be two perfectly valid perspectives—although ironically, even those who write about the Eshu story can't agree on the color of the hat! A perusal of websites on the story include these hat-color combinations: red and white, red and green, red and blue. To make matters more complicated—and humorous—Eshu's traditional colors in Yoruba folklore are red and black. So, if we're still disagreeing about the color of the hat, it appears the trickster is showing us through the Internet sites that we have yet to learn the lessons of Eshu's hat.

Imagine that you feel so certain about a matter that you become upset and angered when someone disagrees with you. You're so confident that you accuse the other person of being crazy or stupid or both. Later, you discover that the person had a good reason for believing the way he did and you apologize or concede that you were acting inappropriately. To your surprise, the other person says the same thing to you. You were both right and both wrong. If that scenario sounds familiar, then you were probably caught in the trickster's trap. You were tricked, but you learned from the experience.

Death and the Trickster

The trickster and the Grim Reaper are known to pal around. When the two come together, they conjure dark irony. You can almost see them laughing and pointing at the mere mortals who are baffled, amused, and sometimes horrified by their work.

At 2:00 A.M. on August 27, 1891, just two miles from Statesville, North Carolina, passenger train number 9 plunged sixty-five feet through a bridge, killing twenty passengers, seriously injuring nine, and leaving twenty other passengers badly bruised and traumatized. This wreck started a ghost-train legend, which says that every year on the anniversary of the wreck, the doomed train returns to haunt the tracks where the mishap occurred. According to an article on WBTV.com, "people have reportedly heard grinding metal, screaming passengers, and a watchman's light." Skip ahead to August 27, 2010. A dozen amateur ghost hunters were on the tracks around 2:45 A.M., hoping to catch sight of the ghost train. As a train came around a curve, the group believed they were seeing the legendary ghost train and that it couldn't hurt them. When they realized the train was real, they started running. All but three people escaped the bridge. A twenty-nine-year-old man was killed, and two others were injured.

This tragic story has the dark trickster's fingerprints all over it. The story also illustrates how the essence of a tragedy often leaves an imprint that echoes up through the centuries. Are the voices of "screaming passengers" and a watchman's light forms of spirit communication? If so, perhaps they serve as warnings. Ironically, the fleeing, screaming ghost hunters were unintentionally mimicking the passengers who had died on the bridge.

The trickster enjoys playing with our perceptions, with irony and synchronicity:

- Will Rogers, humorist, actor, and writer, died in a plane crash with his aviator buddy, Wiley Post, shortly after taking off from a lagoon in Point Barrow, Alaska. Rogers's typewriter was found in the debris—the last word he typed was "death." Even Rogers probably got a kick out of that one.

- Hours after famed Trappist monk Thomas Merton proclaimed to an important meeting of religious leaders that the times ahead were electrifying, he died by electrocution while sitting in the bathtub. Could it be that the trickster—like other archetypes—works through the law of attraction? Or is it the soul—the spirit of the individual—that decides to depart existence on a particular note? Is it both or something else altogether?

- Jim Fixx, whose 1977 bestseller, *The Complete Book of Running*, triggered the jogging craze, died of a heart attack while running. The irony here, of course, is that Fixx died doing what he enjoyed. Is there any better way to go?

- James Heselden, who bought the Segway company, died when he drove his Segway over a thirty-foot cliff on his property and into the river below. In this story, as in the Fixx and Merton examples, the trickster may be the voice of the individual's spirit addressing those of us who are still alive: *Hey, get a load of this. Who's in charge?* The irony grabs our attention and prompts us to question the nature of our beliefs.

Some trickster synchronicities smack of precognition. Take a look:

- The last movie that John Huston directed before his death was called *The Dead*.
- The last book of poetry that Anne Sexton published before she committed suicide in 1974 was entitled *The Death Notebooks*.
- At the time of his death, Philip K. Dick was working on a novel entitled *The Owl in Daylight*. In esoteric traditions, the owl is considered to be a messenger between the living and the dead.
- The last song that Hank Williams Sr. wrote was *Angel of Death*. When he died, he had a hit single at the top of the charts: *I'll Never Get Out of This World Alive*.
- The night before Sugar Ray Robinson fought Jimmy Doyle in 1947, he dreamed he killed his opponent with a single left hook. According to ESPN's Larry Schwartz, Robinson was so shaken by the dream that the next morning he said he couldn't fight Doyle. "But the promoters brought in a Catholic priest who assured Robinson his fears were unfounded. Robinson hit Doyle with a textbook left hook in the eighth round. Doyle was carried from the ring on a stretcher and died the next day."

These types of precognitive synchronicities certainly do illuminate the nature of the trickster spirit.

THE DARK SIDE

Natalie Thomas alerted us to a trickster story that addresses its darker aspects. Recently, two midwives were run over a couple of blocks from Natalie's house by a woman in a van that carried sanitary dispensing units for businesses—i.e., sanitary napkins that are sold through machines in commercial businesses. "The bringers of life were killed by a woman who managed the other end of the fertilization cycle. It was gruesome and otherworldly, and a completely freak accident that no one can explain."

Mythic Element

Whether you believe the events in your life are thrust on you or that you're creating them from the inside out, you're living out a story. We all are. We're the protagonists in our own lives. We're on a journey.

Sometimes, the trickster's job is to sweep us into this mythic landscape, and it doesn't necessarily do this gently. Since this archetype is one of strange contrasts, it holds the light and the dark, the humorous and the tragic, and can trigger shock and awe, as it did for a Swedish woman named Ann who commented on our blog about the death of two family members only a day apart. There didn't appear to be any trickster element involved or even a synchronicity, but the timing of the deaths prompted Ann to note: "The synchronicities of the world can be really cruel. Is it possible to transform such a horrible experience to something good, and start trusting the universe again?"

Her question is certainly valid. When you experience a double whammy like this, your spiritual beliefs are challenged, the way you understand the world is altered, and you're grasping for answers.

Mike Perry of Cornwall, England, responded to Ann. "I know from personal experience how heartbreaking it is when we lose several people in a short time frame. It's hard for us, the ones left behind, but for the people we have 'lost,' it's just a transition. One day we will be linked with them once more and, hopefully, they will be at peace and away from any problems and difficulties they may have had while here on Earth. Meanwhile, there are probably others who need us here at this time, and there are things for us to complete."

A former hospice nurse offered a philosophical and spiritual response to Ann. She said there's always a divine plan at work behind the scenes, and our journeys evolve according to those plans, even when we are too blinded by grief to consider the bigger picture. "And there *is* a bigger picture. Sometimes when we lose several loved ones simultaneously, it's because those souls need and want to be together, even if they may not have seemed connected here. Try to have faith in the plan, even though you don't know what that plan is."

In other words, trust that the souls of your loved ones are following their journey, and know that they are with you in spirit. It's not the same as their physical presence, but it's a comfort. There are lessons in every incident and our paths unfold as we move through the experiences, even those experiences that bring such pain.

Dealing with the Trickster

Now that you've seen these examples, can you think of any events in your life where the trickster manifested? Possibly, it was a shocking synchronicity. For example, Swedish novelist Stieg Larsson, author of *The Girl with the Dragon Tattoo,* completed the manuscript of that novel and two sequels, took all three manuscripts to a publisher, and promptly died. The novels went on to become international bestsellers and popular movies. Larsson never saw his novels published, and his long-time partner, Eva Gabrielsson, not only lost the person closest to her, but she didn't inherit any of the money earned by the novels.

Take a few moments to think about the event and how it affected you, and how you relate to it now. Maybe it was nothing as dramatic as the Stieg Larsson story, but it involved you, and that makes it significant in your life.

1. How did you react?

   a. Were you angry, confused, upset? Did you rail against the universe for being cruel and unfair? Do you still feel that way? Do you live with the loss as a permanent condition, like a widow who only wears black in public?
   b. Were you temporarily sad and at a loss? Did you gradually accept the changed circumstances and adapt to a new reality?
   c. Were people you know surprised by how quickly you accepted the changes in your life? Do you see a larger picture or higher order behind the events?

2. How did you relate to the trickster element in the event?

   a. It was ironic, but not something I ever thought about.
   b. It was on my mind for a long time. I still think about it and wonder what it means.
   c. The trickster element is proof for me that the universe can be cruel and dangerous.

d. The trickster woke me up to the larger picture and my place in it.

e. I can see how some people might think that the trickster is a demon, but I learned a lesson from the experience and have moved on to a new phase in my life.

The Trickster Spirit

When you think of the trickster, you might be thinking of a phenomenon—an event with a striking and ironic synchronicity attached to it—but there are also trickster spirits that can play annoying or disturbing games with us. Such an encounter can be as subtle as the mysterious disappearance of an object that reappears right where you remember leaving it, though you were certain that you'd looked there several times. Other times, an incident might come at you forcefully with an in-your-face attitude, a dramatic incident that literally jolts you into a state of surprise and confusion and, sometimes, into a state of heightened awareness.

These encounters can be startling and frightening, as the following story that involves a trickster spirit who apparently attached himself to a young teenage boy. Although you could label the events in this case as poltergeist experiences—telekinetic experiences often generated by children in puberty—Diana D. of Georgia is convinced that a trickster was feeding on her son's excessive energy and turned it against the family.

At thirteen, Dan was diagnosed with attention deficit disorder. Like many ADHD kids, he was both brilliant and super hyper. He was off his Ritalin when the incidents began. "We had a Ouija board, and Dan wanted to use it. I agreed, and the two of us tried to get some messages."

Diana, a practicing Wiccan, said she invokes every protective technique imaginable before beginning any kind of spiritual activity. However, she believes that a trickster spirit hitched a ride onto Dan's energy field and began to create preternatural incidents, including a disembodied dog that barked and created a spot of urine that appeared in the middle of the bedspread in the master bedroom. The spirit continued to make its presence known through noxious, sickening odors, by moving things, and by making a racket.

One morning after Diana's husband had left for work and the boys were in school, the final incident took place. She was at end of their long, ranch-style house when she heard a sound from the opposite side of the house that sounded like a bomb exploding. "I went flying in there and found all the book-shelves had literally been ripped from the walls." Her collection of crystals, candles and holders, incense, and all of her metaphysical and spiritual books were scattered everywhere.

She was astonished by the power required to pull down the eighteen-foot-long bookshelf, which had been anchored into the wood paneling with three-inch screws. "A grown man could've chinned himself on one of those shelves and it would have held."

She was terrified. Throughout her life, she had done soul rescue work related to hauntings and had been involved in all sorts of high strangeness, "but never anything as wicked and terrifying as this incident."

As she cleaned up the mess, she became convinced that the same malicious spirit that had attached to her son was responsible for the attack. She called her teacher and mentor, whom she refers to as a powerful medium.

Her mentor quickly detected that the trickster was an angry teenage kid stuck in between here and there, who was pulling energy from Dan. The kid had a dog with him. He mentioned the dog before Diana told him about the barking and urinating. "He took care of the discarnate problem child, banished him, sent him to the other side, I guess. We never had another problem after my mentor stepped in and took care of it."

Diana said she learned a great deal from that experience, especially to be cautious when opening doors to worlds we may not know exist. "Many would call this a poltergeist experience. It wasn't. It was a real soul, trapped between dimensions, and living vicariously through my adolescent ADHD son and using his energy to manifest in the physical world."

In spite of the frightening scenario, the apparently troubled lost soul did what tricksters are known to do. The young spirit created strife, testing Diana's strength and resolve, and in the end, she learned an important lesson.

Conjuring Philip

Here's a spirit trickster tale in which the trickster out-tricked the tricksters who created it. Sound complicated? Well, it takes some explaining. We start with a group of nine friends who decided to create their own ghost to see what would happen if they tried to communicate with it.

The group crafted their ghost in great detail, each one taking turn to add elements to the character they called Philip. They described him as an aristocratic Englishman living in the seventeenth century during the time of Oliver Cromwell, and married to a heartless, selfish wife named Dorothea. They gave Philip a mistress, a raven-haired gypsy girl named Margo. They created his likes and dislikes and included some details about historical events of the time that were intentionally inaccurate.

They did so as a spoof to see if their self-created character would accept historical inaccuracies, another way of showing that Philip wasn't an independent spirit.

In their attempt to conjure Philip, the group began meeting weekly in Toronto. They sat around a table with their hands flat on the surface and waited for a response. A year passed with no results, and the group was on the verge of breaking up when one of them discovered that a similar experiment had taken place in England. The English group, however, had followed the method from some of the most successful Victorian-era séances. Instead of sitting quietly and waiting for a reaction from the spirit world, they chatted among each other, telling jokes and thoroughly enjoying themselves. The English group reported successful results, hearing raps coming from the table. The Philip group, feeling they had nothing to lose, decided to copy the technique.

To their surprise, loud knocks soon emanated from the surface of the table. They established a yes-no code—one rap for yes, two for no—and were able to communicate. Philip's answers confirmed the personality they had created. When his wife, Dorothea, was mentioned, Philip would display his distaste by making a scratching sound across the bottom of the table instead of rapping.

Philip adhered to the implanted historical inaccuracies, but he also showed some individuality or rebellion. Even though the group had agreed that Philip loved his mistress, Margo, Philip denied it. He also added aspects to his character—that he enjoyed hunting and shot deer with a musket, that his parents had died of smallpox, that he had worked as a spy for King Charles I.

Philip also exhibited moodiness and didn't like being ignored when members of the group started talking among each other. He liked some members of the group more than others. He enjoyed jokes, liked some songs the group sang, and disliked others. He also didn't like being repeatedly questioned on a subject and would slow his responses and eventually stopped responding altogether when he was annoyed by the direction of the questioning.

Besides rapping, Philip could move or tip the table and move other objects, such as a pitcher of lemonade, across the table. He also performed for television cameras for Canadian documentaries and enjoyed his fifteen minutes of fame. Philip showed himself to be both dependent on the minds of his creators and yet more than the sum of its parts.

Throughout their experiment, the group never considered Philip to be a genuine spirit, but an amalgam of their subconscious minds. In a sense, the members of the group were tricksters creating a false spirit. Yet, Philip tricked the tricksters by moving beyond the limitations of their description of him.

Ultimately, it seems to us, Philip was a spirit who had incorporated the defining characteristics the group created for him. He was both a creation of the group mind and an independent entity playing along.

The trickster, indeed.

The Ouija Trickster

Probably the quickest way to encounter a trickster spirit is to whip out a Ouija board, find a willing partner, and ask if anyone is available to talk. We've written more about Ouija boards in Chapter 12, and you might take a look at that section before you experiment with the board, especially if it's your first time.

That said, keep in mind that the answers you receive from your questions might come from a playful spirit willing to take you on a wild goose chase, especially if you inquire about the nature of the spirit you've contacted. Once the planchette is moving and spelling out words, ask for the name of the spirit. Try to get a full name and a life history—when the person died, where he or she lived, including the exact address, what he or she did for a living, the names of siblings and relatives. Gather as many details as possible. Sometimes the Ouija spirit will provide an amazing amount of information. But is any of it true? Don't count on it.

Thanks to the Internet, you don't need to hire a private detective to look for records related to a deceased person. Plenty of information can be found by following up on what you obtained. Enter the person's name in Google and add the name of the city or town where he or she lived. If you have an address, enter it and you'll find out if it's a real address. If the person supposedly died in a plane crash on a particular date and you know the location, the National Transportation Safety Board investigates all plane crashes and their records are public and available on the Internet. More digging can turn up a list of names of passengers who died.

Maybe you'll actually validate the information you received through the Ouija board, but there's a much better chance that you'll find a trickster chuckling at your efforts. However, if you're unable to verify the identity of a spirit contact, it doesn't mean the contact isn't real. Accuracy is one thing; contact another.

Soon after we met, we tried a Ouija board. The entity that came through claimed to be an alien named Adehe. We immediately asked for proof, and were told that there would be a UFO sighting near the airport late that night. On a whim, we drove to the Fort Lauderdale International Airport, parked, and watched the skies until 2:00 A.M. Nothing happened, and we were both exhausted at work the next morning.

However, later that morning, Rob was on deadline for a story at the daily newspaper where he worked. The reporter at the adjacent desk was also on deadline. When Rob sent off his story to the editor, he asked the other reporter what she was working on. "A UFO story. Broward deputies saw a UFO last night hovering above Perry Airport."

That airport was located ten miles from the airport where we had sat watching for a UFO. The story about the sighting appeared on the front page of the newspaper. It was a synchronicity, but also a frustrating trickster encounter.

Later that evening, we went to Perry Airport and watched the sky. Again, nothing happened. But on the way home, Rob turned on the radio to hear a modern spinoff of the old dramas that dominated radio before television. To his astonishment, this particular drama featured an extraterrestrial being.

Another trickster synchronicity. Was the scenario actual contact with an alien, a spirit being, something else? The deeper that contact stories are explored, the more it seems that the so-called alien visitors appear to come from another dimension, rather than another planet. They might even reside in realms similar to the afterlife. As outrageous and far-fetched as the idea might seem, the mysterious vessels that move at exotic speeds and take impossible turns might be one of the domains of the trickster.

The trickster wakes you up to the larger picture and your place in it. Typically, you are drawn into a bizarre or tragic scenario that might leave you angry or sad. You might rail against the universe for being cruel and unfair, but ultimately, you see a higher order behind events, and that's the trickster's lesson.

11

ANIMALS ATTUNED

Any pet owner will tell you that animals are attuned to what humans can't see, hear, touch, taste, or feel. Animals predict earthquakes and other natural disasters, often act as vehicles for spirit contact, and can sometimes sense illness and even the approach of death in humans.

When Caroline was a hospice nurse, she cared for a coma-tose elderly man who didn't have any relatives or friends. His closest companion was a wolf that lay curled in a corner of the small room where the man's hospital bed was located. It was an unnerving situation.

Since the man was terminal and his transition imminent, she administered palliative care—while the wolf emitted warn-ing growls and snarls. Every so often, the man groaned in pain, and Caroline had to touch him in order to give him injections. As she did so, she kept talking softly to the wolf, explaining that she was helping his human friend. Eventually, the wolf stopped growling whenever she stepped closer to the man.

Shortly before the man died, the wolf stood up and walked over to the bed, which had been elevated so Caroline could tend to him more easily. As the man took his final breath, "his wolf put his paws up on the railing, and stretched so that his paws and chin touched the man's chest." The wolf stayed that way for a while and Caroline didn't interfere. "Then this magnificent ani-mal raised his head and gave the most heart-shattering howl I've ever heard in my life. It was the most poignant experience I had during my years with hospice."

British biologist Rupert Sheldrake has delved into the nature of animals and consciousness for several decades. In *Dogs That Know When Their Owners Are Coming Home and Other Unexplained Powers of Animals,* he cites stories of other cats, dogs, even rabbits who can predict seizures, diabetes, heart attacks, cancer, medical emergencies, and sudden deaths. He even has one case about a dog that appears to have prevented its owner from committing suicide.

The anticipation by animals, particularly dogs, of epileptic fits in their humans is one area where some research has been conducted. "Most dogs that give warning to their owners do so spontaneously and not as a result of any special training. Some dogs give their warning only a few minutes in advance; others can alert their owners half an hour or more before the attack," Sheldrake writes.

Dogs can be trained to respond to seizures, but not to predict them. Yet, among those dogs who can predict, a variety of behaviors are used to warn the owner. The dogs pull on the owner's clothes, bark, or try to pull the owner to a chair or some other safe spot so he or she won't be injured when the seizure begins.

"How is it that animals can be so beneficial to humans?" Sheldrake writes. "The secret of this healing power seems to be the same whether it comes from people or from animals: unconditional love."

This unconditional love and the mysterious bond that is shared between humans and animals may explain why animals are often vehicles for spirit communication. But before we get into that, let's look at your personal relationship with animals.

You and Animals

There are no right and wrong answers. The questions are merely intended to move your thinking in a particular direction.

- Did you have pets as a kid? What kinds of pets? Were they companions or just there?
- What attitude do your parents and siblings have toward animals?
- Are you or anyone in your family an animal activist?
- Are you or anyone in your family a vegan? If so, why? For health reasons? Ethical reasons?

- Do you have pets now?
- What do you think of zoos? Of wildlife refuges? Of dolphins in captivity?
- Do you consider pets as chattel or as companions?
- What role do animals play in your life now? What are your beliefs about animals? Do their souls survive death? Do they reincarnate?
- If you or your children have allergies that prevent you from owning a cat or a dog, have you considered other kinds of pets?
- Do you have a totem animal that is special to you for some reason?
- Do you believe that animals have souls?
- Do you think animals can act as spirit messengers?

Animals as Spirit Messengers

The stories are numerous, but the larger picture is remarkably consistent. A loved one passes away and the family and friends left behind begin to see a particular animal that reminds them of the person who died. Maybe the person had an affinity for this animal or the animal's appearance reflects an internal or external condition that's going on in your life at the time. The message is clear to the people who see the animal: it's the way the deceased is speaking to them from the afterlife.

One man who lost his closest friend was amazed to see a butterfly touch down on his friend's coffin as it was carried into the church. The butterfly remained on top of the coffin throughout the service. Afterward, his widow said to the vicar, "I told you he loved nature."

In some esoteric traditions, butterflies are symbols of transformation. And because there's no greater or more profound transformation than death and rebirth, the man found comfort in the butterfly's behavior. One possible interpretation, in fact, might be that his friend would be reborn soon.

This kind of occurrence is more common than you might think and happens regardless of where you live—bustling city, peaceful countryside, suburbs, a boat, a house on stilts. You're surrounded by wildlife. Even when you're not attuned to animals, they're attuned to you.

Sometimes when you have an experience with an animal, you may have to research the esoteric meaning. Let's say that for several days in a row, a dragonfly flits past your face, touches down on the back of your hand, rests on the roof of your car. You seem to be seeing them everywhere. With your curiosity piqued, you start researching. You discover several esoteric meanings for a dragonfly—illusion, dreams, magic, messenger. You dig more deeply, into folklore and fairy tales about the dragonfly, into its life cycle, how it's regarded in different countries. You begin to develop your own definition for this creature. Then several days after these experiences begin, an event occurs and you suddenly understand what all these dragonflies were telling you.

The event can be anything: you win the lottery, lose your job, fall in love, sell your home, or hear of a friend's death. Now you have direct experience to help you define what your next encounter with a dragonfly might mean. It doesn't necessarily mean this event will be repeated every time you see a dragonfly. But you'll know the dragonfly is alerting you that something is headed your way.

Animals and Synchronicity

The clearest type of spirit communication through an animal occurs when the animal's appearance is a reflection of an internal situation or condition—in other words, a synchronicity. A few days before Easter, an Atlanta couple went to the cemetery to place flowers on the graves of the man's parents. It's a large cemetery located on a busy street, adjacent to Atlanta's busy international airport, without any ponds, creeks, or grain fields nearby that might attract waterfowl or other wildlife.

A pair of Canada geese waddled around the parents' gravesite with great purpose. "With no water, food, or other attractant in the vicinity, this was strangely comical—sort of like finding a buffalo or aardvark wandering around a mausoleum—it struck me as that incongruous," the man said. The two geese stayed nearby as the couple arranged the flowers on the headstone.

As they drove away a while later, he remembered that Canada geese mate for life. The symbolism struck him. His parents spent nearly their entire adult lives together. After his father's death, his grieving mother lasted only six months. "This pair of geese: were they there that day to honor my parents' memory?" he asked. "I saw them as a fitting tribute at Easter for my folks, a devoted couple."

It's also possible that the geese were a message from his parents, letting him know they are together again in the hereafter.

Animal attunement and synchronicity that involve death can change you. Somehow, your view of the universe and your role in it are seen from a much larger perspective. It's as if you suddenly have an eagle's view and can discern connections that eluded you before.

Birds and Spirit Contact

We've noticed that birds seem to figure prominently in many synchronicities that involve spirit contact. Perhaps it's simply that birds are so numerous—there are more than 9,000 species found on every continent, including Antarctica. But even in mythology, folklore, fairy tales, and religion, birds play important roles. They are found in creation myths, are often viewed as messengers of the gods, appear as tricksters, and are used in oracles. Some types of birds, like ravens, are regarded in myths as symbolic of war and misfortune, but also as mediators between humans and the supernatural world.

In esoteric traditions, crows are, among other things, messengers. Sometimes they are messengers of death—not yours, but the death of someone else. The term "murder of crows" may have originated from a fallacious folktale that crows form tribunals to judge and punish the bad behavior of a member of the flock. If the verdict goes against the defendant, that bird is killed—murdered—by the flock. The basis is probably that crows sometimes will kill a dying crow that doesn't belong in their territory or feed on the carcasses of dead crows.

On August 28, 2009, in West Palm Beach, an eighteen-year-old man awaited the verdict on the crimes with which he was charged—fourteen felonies that included burglary, kidnapping, five counts of sexual battery with great force, and the savage act of forcing a mother and son into sexual acts together. He was one of ten youths involved in the ruthless assault and gang rape against the thirty-seven-year-old woman and her twelve-year-old son, a crime that shocked the community for its brutality. Moments before the verdict was read, a murder of crows hovered outside the windows of the courtroom, filling the gray sky.

The reckoning came with the crows. Nathan Walker and another defendant were convicted of eleven felonies. Walker now faces life in prison, which is certainly a kind of death, by any standard.

In some cultures, birds are associated with birth. The connection of babies with storks may have originated centuries ago in northern Germany, and remnants survive to the present day. In folklore and cartoons, for instance, storks are often depicted delivering a bundled baby to a doorstep or bringing it down through a chimney. Young children who ask where babies come from are sometimes told the stork delivers them.

In other cultures, birds are also associated with the soul's journey after death, with resurrection and rebirth, and with immortality. And any bird may play that role.

While Betty's father was hospitalized and not expected to live, a little bluebird sat on the windowsill outside his room, singing and singing. Her father loved birds and could imitate many of their songs and sounds. Even late that evening, when a thunderstorm came, the little bluebird continued to sit on the hospital windowsill, singing. It stayed there until the moment her father died—and then flew away. "My mother always believed the bluebird came to accompany him on his journey out of the body," says Betty.

In fact, once you delve into the roles of birds in mythology and folklore, you'll begin noticing how they're used in fairy tales, cartoons, books, and movies. In the Harry Potter books, owls deliver the mail to Hogwarts. In the movie, that mail delivery scene leaped to life when all the owls swept into the massive dining room and letters rained down. In J. R. R. Tolkien's *Lord of the Rings*, the Great Eagles were huge gold eagles that were wise and could speak. In the movie version, the Great Eagles were 20 feet tall, with tremendous wingspans. In *Blade Runner*, based on a Philip K. Dick short story ("Do Androids Dream of Electric Sheep?"), birds are a recurring motif used to depict freedom—and imprisonment. You get the idea here: Birds as symbols are a part of our collective unconscious.

WILD PARROTS, SYNCHRONICITY, AND SPIRIT CONTACT

Darren, who lives in Brisbane, Australia, related an intriguing synchronicity involving wild parrots and spirit contact. His father-in-law, John, enjoyed feeding wild parrots, magpies, kookaburras, and other birds that would drop by his house daily, actually sitting on the veranda railing, waiting to be fed.

"John enjoyed watching parrots doing their mating dance, and would sometimes imitate the male parrot, which wobbles up behind the female and then flaps its wings up and down—a bit like a dirty old man flapping his raincoat. It would send him into hysterics."

Even though John didn't believe in life after death, Darren said he often joked about coming back as a parrot.

On the day after he died suddenly and unexpectedly of a heart attack, Darren's mother-in-law turned on the TV, hoping to distract herself from her grief. She tuned in to *Australia's Funniest Home Videos*. "And what should come on? Two parrots trying their mating dance out on an artificial parrot. What are the odds?"

Darren said that even though his wife and mother-in-law don't believe in an afterlife, they were struck by the synchronicity and found great comfort it. He hopes it opens their minds to the possibility of an afterlife.

Your Messengers

This activity requires you to become an archeologist of your own life, specifically of your memories. So let's start with the simple stuff.

- Think back. Have you had at least one experience with meaningful coincidence—synchronicity—that involved animals? When we asked friends this question, the results intrigued us. Everyone had a different take on a hummingbird. Or a domestic cat. Or a pet dog. Or a wild hawk. And that's the point. You distill your experiences with a particular animal in a way that fits your world-view, beliefs, experiences. There's also a collective level to these experiences that you can explore through mythology, cultural and religious beliefs, and folklore.
- What were the animals? You may discover that some of your most powerful synchronicities involve the same type of animal or species.
- Start a journal about these experiences. If you already have a journal, then begin compiling your own animal dictionary. Tap into folklore and mythology to help you define the meanings of these animals. This is basically what Trish did in *Animal Totems: The Power and Prophecy of Your Animal Guides*, where she and coauthor Millie Gemondo compiled esoteric meanings of animals. The end result, though, should be your own meanings, based on your own experiences and research.
- Your meanings can be gleaned from dreams, too. With dream symbolism, pay close attention not only to the animals but to their colors, behaviors, and actions in the dream. Jenean Gilstrap dreamed she was walking

along a concrete walkway with a ledge that overlooked a large body of water. Walking on the ledge were two animals, almost "totem" in their appearance—a blue bear and a blue lion. She wasn't frightened by these animals, but knew they were out of place and felt they weren't personal symbols, but were of a collective nature. The ledge and other symbols in the dream pointed to some sort of global shift in consciousness that would bring the world into a more peaceful and balanced place. Writing from late 2010, this obviously hasn't happened yet, but it's interesting to note that animal symbolism raises our collective awareness in surprising ways, as you'll see in a story later in this chapter concerning a woman and a dolphin.

- Be sure to date your journal entries. This could prove to be valuable later when you encounter a skeptic. Or when you become your own worst critic.
- As your collection of definitions grows, expand on it by talking to others about their experiences. There are plenty of sites and blogs on the Internet about the symbolic meanings of animals. Also, drop by our blog on synchronicity—*www.synchrosecrets.com/synchrosecrets*—where we've posted many stories about synchronicity and spirit contact.

The Spirits of Pets

A universal synchronicity involving spirit contact occurs with our beloved pets that have passed on. The experiences differ from pet to pet, of course, and also vary according to the species, but an overall pattern prevails.

You might, for instance, hear or smell something that reminds you of your dog or cat. Judi Hertling sometimes catches a wet-dog smell in her room, meaningful to her because her German shepherd, Sheba, loved swimming in the ocean. Or you might feel the pet jump onto the foot of your bed at night. There could even be a visible depression in the mattress. Your pet may come to you through a dream, a vision, or even as an image when you're meditating or relaxing.

If you have other pets, they may pick up on the visitation before you do. Animals that have lived together often mourn the loss of their buddies, and can be the first to let you know you're being visited.

The spirits of animals, like those of humans, sometimes do surprising things to communicate with us. Jennifer L. had a malamute, Dakota, whom she loved dearly. "She was very wolfish but also very human and intuitive in amazing ways. I always felt she bridged the gap between the human world and the world of nature for me. She was my best friend for so many years and after she passed, I could feel her presence for a long time. Then I stopped feeling her around. That made me sad."

About nine months after her death, she came home one day and saw Dakota's paw print on the window. "It was exactly what she loved to do: jump on the window to look out. Now whenever I miss her, I think of that and feel comforted."

We have heard of handprints and initials on frosted or steamed windows as vehicles of communication from human spirits, but this is a first for a paw print!

Kids are more intuitively open to these kinds of experiences. Vicki DeLaurentis recalls hearing her daughter talking one night in her room. She went in to check on her and was about to sit on the bed when her daughter shouted, "No, mommy, not there!"

Vicki, taken back, asked why she couldn't sit on the bed. Her daughter replied that Zachary, the family dog who had recently died, always sat on the bed when he came to see her. She said that he liked to be with her and usually stayed until she fell asleep.

Whether our pets visit in dreams or in waking life, they seem to do so for many of the same reasons that human loved ones drop by: for companionship, to let us know they're fine, to bring insights and information, and to comfort us. And sometimes they visit to let us know they're moving on.

Years ago, we had a one-eyed Himalayan cat named Demian, after the novel by Herman Hesse. His blind left eye was the result of a claw piercing the retina before we had him. He still had the eye, but it was a soft, milky color. Trish had gotten him from an animal control shelter when she was in graduate school and he moved around the country with her until she settled in Fort Lauderdale, where she and Rob met. Rob nicknamed him Doolittle, because he really didn't do much, but he sure was lovable. He was a part of Trish's life for fourteen years, her dependable buddy through major transitions. When his kidneys failed, we had to put him to sleep.

About four months after that dark, bleak day of his death, Trish dreamed that she came downstairs to the kitchen to get a bite to eat and there was Doolittle, munching away at his cat food. In the dream, she said, "Doolittle, how can you be here? You're dead."

He looked up at her with that single beautiful blue eye. "No, I'm not. Not really. I'm coming back. You'll recognize me."

That was more than twenty years ago, and she hasn't dreamed of him since. In the late 1990s, we adopted Jessie, a two-year-old golden retriever. When we took her to the vet for shots, the vet said she had scar tissue in the retina of her left eye, but that it didn't affect her vision.

Doolittle was blind in his left eye. We like to think that the synchronicity was confirmation that Doolittle really had returned.

Animals as Archetypes

If we look at animals as archetypes, then when you have a synchronistic experience with an animal, the archetype has become active within your psyche. It may stay active for years. The same thing is true for archetypes that become active in the collective psyches of a community, country, or the planet.

The Deepwater Horizon disaster in the Gulf of Mexico in the spring of 2010 reached a tipping point when the media began releasing photos of oil-slicked birds, dead fish, and dolphins floundering and dying. The archetype of an endangered planetary environment became active in our collective psyche. People started to demand answers; the BP CEO was forced to step down; Congress held hearings; Americans were disgusted, enraged. They had been seized by the archetype of death in the Gulf.

At the collective level, symbols speak to the larger picture of a community, society, state, or country. They speak to nature, the planet, the universe. In modern times, then, the extinction of a species might be addressing the precarious fragility of our ecosystem. A disaster like the earthquake and tsunami in Indonesia in 2004, in which so few animals were killed, could be alerting us to the importance of paying closer attention to our instincts in order to survive climate change.

"The Self is often symbolized as an animal, representing our instinctive nature and its connectedness with one's surroundings," wrote M. L. von Franz in *Man and his Symbols*, a collection of essays that Carl Jung edited. "This is why there are so many helpful animals in myths and fairy tales." He was referring to animal symbols in dreams, but his words pertain to waking life as well. "This relation of the Self to all surrounding nature and even the cosmos probably comes from the fact that the 'nuclear atom' of our psyche is somehow woven into the whole world, both outer and inner."

Doesn't it sound a lot like David Bohm's belief that everything in the universe unfolds from an inner order?

But there are also times when the humans come to the aid of animals and we should strive to decipher that message as well.

The March 11, 2011, disasters in Japan—a 9.0 earthquake, tsunami, intense aftershocks, and subsequent nuclear meltdown devastated the country. In the weeks after the disaster, we couldn't find much information about how animals had fared. Then one afternoon, a friend in Hawaii asked if we had heard about the tsunami dolphin. We hadn't and Vivian, whom we had met because of our mutual interest in dolphins, suggested we Google it.

According to the *Christian Science Monitor*, a group of volunteers in Japan had been searching for and rescuing abandoned animals. One of the volunteers received a call from Masayuki Sato about a stranded dolphin in the rice fields.

But what Sato thought was a dolphin turned out to be a baby porpoise. The group tried to catch the little porpoise with a net, but to no avail. So Ryo Taira, a pet store owner, moved out into the shallow water and scooped the porpoise up into his arms. Due to the extensive damage in the area, they didn't have an aquarium they could take the porpoise to, so they wrapped it in wet towels and drove it a mile to the coast.

There, they set the baby porpoise free. Taira said the little guy perked up when it was returned to the water. "I don't know if it will live," he told the *Asahi Shimbun* newspaper. "But it's certainly a lot better than dying in a rice paddy."

So what is this baby porpoise telling us? Perhaps its message is that in the midst of profound chaos and pain, compassion and hope have been born and flourish. We are all one.

What archetypes are active in your psyche?

When a Dying Animal Reaches Out to You

If animals act as spirit contacts for us, then isn't it possible that animals sometimes need and seek out human contact before they pass on? If you've had pets throughout your life, you probably have faced, at least once, the terrible and heartbreaking experience of putting your pet to sleep.

Many pet owners in that situation report that as the injection begins to take effect, the animal is acutely aware of what's happening and reaches out to connect in some way. The dog or cat reaches out with its paw, licks your hand, locks eyes with you. Sometimes, you can see your pet's soul as it leaves its body, a pale wisp, like smoke. Years ago, an elderly friend who had never married and didn't have children, owned a lovebird that was the center of her world. When that bird died, she was holding it in her hands and saw its soul leave through the top of the little bird's head. It looked like mist.

Experiencing this kind of event with a pet who has been a member of your family is one thing. Experiencing this with an animal in the wild is something else. Just ask Renee Prince.

Since she was twenty-one, Renee was obsessed with dolphins and wanted to study interspecies communication. She earned a master's degree in experimental psychology so she could study dolphin cognition, hoping it would lead to some sort of mutual communication system between their species and ours.

For years, she worked with orcas and dolphins in captivity. "But I came to realize that life in the tanks is ultimately an early death sentence for dolphins, and the brief life they do have is impoverished and intolerable." After two of her dolphins died, Renee left dolphin research. She just couldn't face another death of one of her "friends," and was powerless to change their situation. "Captive dolphins and whales are, to the rest of the world, simply property to be sold, used, and disposed of quickly when they no longer can serve human purposes. Since then I've lived with the guilt and pain of having left the dolphins behind."

Decades later, after she had changed careers to work in the film business, she lived next to the beach in the hopes of seeing dolphins. She often jogged along the shore, always looking past the waves for the telltale arcs of fins or exhalations that meant dolphins were once again visiting her section of the beach. She would see them once in a while and would rush out to meet them, hoping they could stay and play.

Late one afternoon, Renee was alone on the beach, jogging, when she noticed a dolphin in the waves. She could tell something was terribly wrong. The surf was washing over him, tumbling him over and over. He was trying to get to shore because he was too weak to keep himself afloat. He was in imminent danger of drowning. Renee ran into the water and pushed out toward him.

"When he saw me, his eyes widened in fear, just for a moment, and then he headed directly toward me. At that second, I had the odd, yet utterly certain feeling that this dolphin had been waiting for me. When we reached each other and I put my arms around him, just as I had always done with my own dolphin friends so many years ago, he relaxed against me and looked up at me with complete trust. I held him upright, keeping his blowhole above water, and he helped us head toward shore, moving his pectoral fins to steer us and slowly pumping his flukes."

They kept in constant eye contact as they moved toward shore. Renee spoke constantly to the dolphin. She promised she wouldn't leave his side, that she would call the marine mammal rescue center, and would ride with him to wherever they could keep him, even if it had to be the place she'd fled long ago. And she promised the dolphin she wouldn't let him be kept captive; she would make sure he was released back into the sea when he was well.

But as they reached the shore, in water only a few inches deep, the dolphin wanted to turn around, to face back out to sea.

"I helped him turn, he came to a stop. He lay back in my arms, looked deeply and calmly into my eyes, and died. I saw the light go out of him. Somehow this dolphin, who never would have been near shore—he was a deep water species, Delphinus delphis—had traveled untold miles away from his world and had, in an utterly alien world, met the only human on this beach who could have seen him, who knew what he wanted and could help him get to shore. He died in the arms of someone who, he must have known, loved him instantly and without conditions; someone who knew dolphins and for years had longed with all her heart for another chance at contact with his kind."

It took Renee a long time to process the encounter. She'd thought she was there to save the dolphin. When that didn't happen, she was horrified and angry at "God, fate, the Tao, myself," she told us in an e-mail. "Was there something I could have done differently or better so that he could have been saved? But I was left with no explanation, only the power and soul-wrenching synchronicity of our encounter. I've since come to believe that my dolphin wanted to die in the presence of love. I gave him that, I'm sure."

What a different sort of world this would be if we humans could love as unconditionally as animals do.

By recognizing that synchronicity is meaningful, you open yourself up to a wondrous universe in which everything seems to be connected. Time and space, distance, even death can't sever those connections. Once you're aware of that, you're more receptive to the idea that animals can be vehicles of synchronicity and spirit contact. And once you're receptive, your experiences will become more frequent and powerful, and you'll become as attuned to animals as they are to you.

12

GUIDING SPIRITS

When you think of spirit guides, what comes to mind? Maybe a deceased grandparent or an ancestor. Possibly, someone from long ago, a Native American shaman, a Roman soldier, or a Greek scholar. How about a guardian angel with wings? You might imagine this benevolent being appearing as a glowing entity resonating powerful protective and supportive energy.

But sometimes guidance from the other side appears as symbols, like the appearance of a white feather, that require interpretation. Such symbols can be puzzling, even annoying, until you recognize them.

One morning outside the gym, we saw at least two dozen crows circling above two tall pine trees, a flock of black birds swirling among them. As we watched the dark maelstrom, we realized our car was parked directly beneath the pine trees. Sure enough, the hood and windshield were splattered with bird droppings. We also noticed that the surrounding cars were somehow spared. Annoyed, we drove away.

On the drive home, our attitude shifted to concern as we remembered that a murder of crows could be interpreted as messengers of death. What could their appearance directly over our car mean? And what about the symbolism of our car covered with bird droppings? By the time we arrived home, we hoped the message related to guiding spirits and the release of a trapped soul. The soul in question was Rob's second cousin, whose death was mentioned in the introduction.

John MacGregor spent thirty years in the army, rising from a private to the rank of colonel. He was in the South Pacific in World War II and later stationed in Korea. After the Korean conflict ended, he worked for years in the Pentagon. Even though, in John's later years, he and Rob lived across the country from each other, they kept in touch by telephone and mail. After learning of his death, Rob expected a dream, a vision, or a vivid impression about John, but none came. That surprised him, since he had experienced such contact with relatives and friends who had passed on.

However, a couple of weeks after John's death, while in a drowsy state, Rob focused on John and asked him where he was. An image surfaced of John as a much younger man, wearing a dress uniform and standing alone at a bar. Rob noticed a door and tried to lead John toward it, but he wouldn't leave.

Rob knew John as a deeply religious man who frowned on what he saw as excessive materialism, especially at Christmas time. Every year he would say that people were missing the point of the holiday, the spiritual aspect. So Rob was baffled by the impression of John being unwilling to move on. Was he now stuck between worlds? If so, what was preventing him from moving ahead?

Rob asked Morgana Starr, a medium in Cocoa Beach, Florida, to tune into John. "He's stuck. He feels that he's not worthy. He has to forgive himself," she said. A year earlier, psychic Millie Gemondo predicted that John would be clinging to this life, that he wouldn't want to let go.

Five weeks after John's death, Rob dreamed that John was still in between worlds and was being visited by two men in suits. Rob felt the men were manipulators, like con artists, perhaps lower astral entities who were trying to persuade John to do something that seemed wrong. The men apparently had visited before, but now they appeared to be aware of Rob and others and were not going to leave John alone. Again, Rob spotted a way out, an opening to another dimension. But John didn't see it. However, it seemed he had a better idea of what was going on. The last word Rob heard, which seemed to come from John, was "trapped."

Another three weeks passed. Rob didn't have any dreams about John, but sensed something was changing. When he meditated on John, he didn't feel the stress that he'd noted earlier. It was as if John had moved on. But he wanted to verify it, so he contacted Jane Clifford, a medium in Wales.

Jane reported that she was able to connect with John quite easily. Even though she doesn't have a Native American spirit guide, she was contacted by a group of them. "It seemed they were only waiting to be asked to help and they responded with great readiness. I am getting a positive assurance that things have already shifted quickly for him. Your intent and involvement has been crucial in facilitating these changes for the highest good of all, including the two manipulative entities, who have been offered the opportunity to transmute into light."

She felt John's gratitude that Rob's timely intervention had finally brought him release from the guilt, anxiety, and unfinished business that had been holding him. "It facilitated self-forgiveness and the release of those vibrations in him that attracted the energies that were keeping him trapped." She saw a symbol, the release of a dove from human hands. She felt it indicated John's spirit was now free and Rob's intent would assist him in traveling on unimpeded.

Native American spirit guides are a common element in mediumistic readings, dating back to the heyday of spiritualism in the early 1900s. The mere mention of a Native American spirit guide leads some people to suspect fakery or fraud. While Jane noted that she doesn't typically deal with such guardian entities, their appearance in this instance seemed synchronistic; John MacGregor had provided generous financial support to Native American causes for many years.

That was only one of the synchronicities related to Jane's efforts on behalf of John. She concluded her reading by suggesting that we look for confirmation through dreams, symbols, and power animals. She also asked if the color purple had any meaning for Rob. In fact, we had just eaten at one of our favorite Asian restaurants, where Rob had ordered sushi.

A purple flower was included as decoration on the plate. As for symbols and power animals, the next morning we saw the crows circling above our car.

An hour after returning home from the gym, Rob went outside to wash the car. The sky sagged with heavy, purple clouds, it started to sprinkle, and before he could pull out the hose, it started pouring. When the storm ended twenty minutes later, the car had been washed clean of bird droppings. The purple sky and the cleansing were the punctuation point at the end of his questions about how John was doing.

A Dream Guide

Sometimes, spirit guides appear in dreams and use symbolism as well as words to present their message. In the following story, a guide appears next to the dreamer in a bus, which represents life's journey.

When Debra Page's husband, Larry, asked her to marry him, they'd known each other for four years. They had met as coworkers at a car dealership. She'd met his father, knew he had a younger brother, and that his mother had died of diabetes-related complications in 1982.

He asked her to marry him on December 12, 1992. She said yes, and Larry moved into an apartment with Debra and her daughter. She knew they were facing a lot of issues resulting from the fact that the marriage was interracial.

A few weeks after they moved in together, Debra had a vivid dream: "I was on a bus in San Diego. My seven-year-old daughter was sitting to my right. On my left was a stranger: an African American woman. She was beautiful, with a dynamic presence. She had an afro—very big hair. She said, 'My name is

Nita. This is going to be very hard for Larry. Please be patient. It will all work out.'"

The next morning, Debra told Larry her dream. He replied that Nita was his mother. Her name was Juanita, but everyone called her Nita, and yes, she had an afro hairdo.

They moved to San Diego in 1993, and stayed a few weeks at Larry's family's home. Debra was home alone, cleaning, when she found a photograph of the woman in her dream: a beautiful black woman with an afro. It was Nita. "Somehow, I knew she would always be looking out for us."

Contacting a Deceased Loved One

If there's a particular person in spirit you would like to contact, your best chance might be through a dream. Before going to bed, look at a photograph of that person or picture the person in your mind. Say his or her name. As you drift off, you may hear a greeting or a message of love and reassurance that all is well. However, be aware that if you're trying to reach a person who has recently died, that spirit might not be capable of serving as a guide. In fact, *you* might act as a guide for the spirit.

Sometimes, a person who has died recently is more aware of living people than spirit beings. You might glimpse the deceased person in an ordinary setting and realize that he or she is unwilling to move on. In such a case, you can direct the soul toward spirit guides who are waiting to help. One way to do that is through prayer.

When Rob's cousin was trapped, Jane Clifford suggested that Rob recite Morrnah's Prayer, a nonreligious prayer of native Hawaiian heritage:

Divine creator, father, mother, son as one. If I, my family, relatives and ancestors have offended you, your family, relatives and ancestors in thoughts, words, deeds and actions from the beginning of our creation to the present, we ask your forgiveness. Let this cleanse, purify, release, cut all the negative memories, blocks, energies and vibrations, and transmute these unwanted energies into pure light. And it is done.

A shorter version is known as the Ho'oponopono mantra and goes like this:

I love you
I am sorry
Please forgive me
Thank you

Powering Up for Contact

Even though some people have exceptional talent to make contact with spirit guides while awake in a meditative state, it's a natural ability, one that can be developed by anyone through patience and practice.

To power up for contact, find a comfortable place to sit, preferably in a reclining chair, at a time when you won't be disturbed. Take several long, slow, deep breaths through your nose, exhale slowly through your mouth. Feel yourself entering a relaxed state.

Imagine that the room around you is no longer visible. Instead, you're surrounded by a crystal dome with windows that look out into a star-studded sky. Your chair is in the center of the dome. Think of this dome as an energy station where you can access higher energy that will resonate through your entire being, raising your awareness and sensitivity.

As you rest back in your chair, light fills the dome with a bright energy that becomes increasingly more intense. Concentrate. See the light forming a ball of intense energy just below your navel, at your second chakra. ("Chakra" is a term from Eastern philosophic and healing practices that refers to the invisible energy centers that run from the base of the spine to the crown of the head.) This chakra, the center of emotions, vitality, fertility, and creativity, is associated with the sex organs. See the light glowing there, expanding. Focus on it, feel the intensity. Feel your body start to vibrate, then release the energy.

When you're ready, form the light into a ball again and move it to your heart chakra, the center of love, healing, compassion. Again, the light intensifies and glows brightly. Hold it there until you feel the vibrations growing stronger, then release it.

Now reform the ball and move it to the crown chakra at the top of your head. This chakra connects you with messages from higher realms. It's where you receive information about your life purpose and spiritual path. See and feel it glowing and expanding. Feel the vibrations intensifying. Hold it as long as you can, then release it in an explosion of light.

Now imagine a ring of light coming down from above your head, moving all the way to your feet. See it move up and down your body, smoothing out the vibrations. Now you're ready to make contact.

Reaffirm that you're inside your crystal dome, where you're protected from any negative energy from lower entities. Say to yourself: "I'm protected, but remain open to contact with spirits of equal or higher vibrational level. Whatever contact is made will be beneficial. Now I'm ready to meet a spirit guide."

How you perceive a spirit guide varies for each of us. You might pick up a scent, an etheric perfume that doesn't exist in the physical world. It could make you feel as if you're about to lift up out of your body. Or you may hear celestial music that fills your being like nothing you've ever heard. Maybe you hear a comforting voice. Later, you might not recall what was said. You might glimpse a spirit guide—a beautiful face—or you might see the entire being, possibly wearing glowing, colorful clothing.

Contact may come in the form of touch. You might feel as if someone has just placed a hand on your shoulder or simply sense that someone is near you. You could experience an emotional reaction to contact, an overwhelming sense of elation, or shed tears of joy.

If it's your first attempt to make contact with a spirit guide, your experience could seem momentary or ephemeral. Know that you can make contact and that, with practice, you can deepen and expand your experience.

JUNG'S SPIRIT GUIDE

Over a three-day period in 1916, Carl Jung channeled a spirit guide, who called himself Basilides. He was an actual person born in Syria, a teacher in Alexandria in 133–155 A.D. Words, thoughts, and ideas came to Jung as Basilides dictated and Jung transcribed. The material was later published as *Sermones ad Mortuos*, or *The Seven Sermons to the Dead*, a collection of commentaries by Basilides to the dead. Many religious teachings tell us that when we die, we will meet the supreme being or at least learn more about God. But in *The Seven Sermons*, the dead come to Basilides for knowledge.

The first line of *Seven Sermons* reads: "The dead came back from Jerusalem, where they found not what they sought. They prayed me let them in and sought my word, and thus I began my teaching." Basilides refers to God as Abraxas, an ancient name.

Basildes's sermons emphasize human individuality. He explains that upon death, we maintain the fullness of our individuality rather than being absorbed into the oneness. It's impossible to say how much of what Jung wrote was from his own unconscious mind and how much, if any, came from an outside source. However, in the aftermath of his experience channeling Basilides, Jung formulated his concept of the collective unconscious. He considered it part of the evolutionary process common to all people, and distinct from individual consciousness. He thought of it as the foundation of what the ancients called sympathy of all things.

Shamanic Journey

While primitive cultures lacked organized religion as we know it today, there was no lack of contact with the other side. Shamanism, the oldest spiritual practice known to mankind, dates back tens of thousands of years. At the heart of the spiritual practice is contact with the ancestors, who reside in the spirit world. Shamanism has experienced a modern revival in Western culture. Numerous books are available on the subject and shamanic workshops are regularly taught by trained instructors.

Think of the shamanic journey as a way of problem solving and gaining knowledge through a spirit guide that might be in human or animal form. Typically, the journey is accompanied by repetitive beats of a drum or the shaking of rattles. If you Google "shamanic drumming," you'll find a selection of available CDs. You can also download fifteen- or thirty-minute selections of shamanic drumming from iTunes for $1. The monotonous beat will help move you into a trance-like state.

In the shamanic journey, there are three worlds—the lower, the middle, and the upper. The Upper World is where you're most likely to meet a teacher or spirit guide in human form. En route, you might pass through a cloud before you emerge into a bright place that might appear as a crystal city that floats without a foundation. The Upper World has many levels that can be explored and can take on numerous images.

To reach the Upper World, you begin in a place of nature. You travel upward, possibly by climbing a ladder or rope leading into the clouds, crawling up a tall tree, rising up in a hot air balloon, soaring to the top of a mountain, or maybe mounting stairways leading to the top of a tower. Before embarking on your journey, think of a question you would like answered.

Look for your spirit guide and pay close attention to what happens. Notice how the guide acts, what he shows you, how he communicates. Keep your question in mind. The answer can come in assorted ways and you may need to interpret your impressions. The message may appear as a metaphor, such as a message to weed your garden. Instead of thinking that you don't have a garden or that it's winter, think of what you can "weed out" of your life.

Talking to a Spirit Guide

Here's a specific route you might try to reach the Upper World. In this method, you are both traveler and observer.

Begin by sitting or lying down in a comfortable, quiet place where you won't be interrupted. Have a clear purpose in mind. Where do you need help in your life? It's best to avoid time-related and yes or no questions, such as, "Should I take this job offer?" Better than a yes or no answer would be a response to the question, "What will I experience if I take this new job?" The answer might be, "You will learn what it's like to work for a little tyrant!"

Start your question with what, who, where, why, or how. *What* do you want to know? It could be a question about your current circumstances: your love life, career, finances, health. You might ask for help with a creative project. Or maybe you have a bigger question: What's my path in life? What's my core issue? Is it fear, self-worth, an emotional block? Why do my relationships keep failing? What do I need to change about my life?

Entering the Upper World

Once you're ready, take several deep breaths, inhaling and exhaling slowly. Feel your body relaxing from the crown of your head, down your face and neck, shoulders and arms, to your hands. Let your chest and back relax, your abdomen, hips, buttocks. Feel the relaxation rolling down your legs, thighs, knees, shins and calves, ankles and feet. Place your hands on your heart and leave the everyday world behind.

When you're relaxed and ready to begin, imagine that you're climbing a winding trail and you look up to see a tower on a hill high above. Dusk is approaching as you move closer. You climb stairs leading up the hill to the entrance of the tower.

After you reach the top step and pause, an elevator door hisses open, and you step inside. You see a panel with an illuminated number 1 that changes to 2 as you rise. Watch the numbers and listen as a soft voice counts slowly upward to ten.

The door opens, you step into a circular chamber and settle into a reclining chair. The walls glow and gradually change colors from red to orange, yellow, green, blue, purple, and violet. Repeat your question. Now you notice a wide screen on the wall, and your guide appears on the screen, like a movie star. Pay attention to the surroundings. What does your guide say and do? The guide might address you from the screen and give you an answer.

Alternately, you might find yourself in the movie with the guide and the two of you venture off. Your answer may lie in wherever you go. Maybe your feelings shift, imparting a message. The answer could come in a combination of feelings, actions, and spoken words.

Tools for Contact

Besides meditation practices and dream encounters, there are tools available that can help you make contact with a spirit guide. It can be as simple as paper and a pen, a Ouija board or something more high-tech, with a recording device.

Automatic Writing

This form of contact leaves behind an impression, words on paper, thoughts from the other side that can be studied and unraveled. In essence, a spirit guide takes over the movement of your hand and writes a message without your awareness of what is being written.

Some people have received detailed messages, even complete novels, through automatic writing. There's no doubt that it's a real phenomenon, but the source of the information is a matter of conjecture. Some people will never acknowledge that contact can be made with spirits. Whether the information comes from your subconscious mind or from a spirit guide is a matter of perspective.

Inspired writing happens when a writer achieves a breakthrough that might involve synchronicity—an incident in the environment that triggers new ideas, a new approach. At all times, the writer is in control of the movement of his or her hand and the words that appear. Automatic writing involves the physical manipulation of the writer's hand.

One of the best times to begin automatic writing is in the aftermath of the death of someone close to you. While such sad events aren't necessary to produce material through automatic writing, you're more emotional and open to making contact during periods of grieving.

Begin by having a notebook and a pen ready. On your first effort don't ask a question, just see what happens. Find a quiet spot free of distractions. Sit at a table or desk so that you can rest your arm. Take several deep breaths, inhaling and exhaling slowly. Focus on your breath, and release your thoughts.

Touch the pen to the paper, hold it firmly, but don't clench the pen. Try not to consciously write anything, just let your hand move and write, even if it seems to be scribbling. Avoid looking at the paper. Notice how you feel as the pen starts to move. Don't be surprised if you feel stimulated or aroused.

When the pen stops moving, take a look at what you have produced. It might look like scribbling. If you don't see any words, look for an image in the scribbles, and see if you can decipher it. If it's meaningful, you've just experienced a synchronicity, possibly related to spirit contact. Now you're ready to ask questions.

On the other hand, if nothing happens after fifteen minutes, take a break or wait for another time. But don't give up; keep trying. It might take several efforts before you succeed. Of course, there's no guarantee that automatic writing will work for you. If, after several tries, nothing comes through, you might team up with a partner and try a Ouija board.

Ouija Board

Using a Ouija board to contact a spirit guide is somewhat similar to buying a used car from a dealer who has the best prices in town, but you know that some of the cars are damaged goods. With a Ouija board, you can communicate with entities of equal or higher vibration than yourself, but you can also get nonsense or threatening comments from mischievous lower entities. That's especially true if you don't take the communication seriously or you're looking for a thrill rather than wisdom and knowledge. It's also why Ouija boards are often maligned as dangerous, and are considered the most controversial method of contacting the other side.

The board is a medium for communication, like automatic writing, but uses a planchette instead of a pen. The board, of course, is not an entity itself and has no power. It's a piece of pressed cardboard. If you don't like what you're getting, stop using it. There's no need to burn the board or bury it, as some have done.

While many who use the Ouija board are convinced it's a vehicle for contact with the other side, skeptics believe the planchette slips around through unconscious muscle movements, that there's nothing otherworldly about it. At the other extreme are people who believe that dabbling with a Ouija board will result in contact with evil forces intent on deception and abuse. Remember that the Ouija board is a tool, nothing more, nothing less. The quality of information you receive depends to some degree on what you expect.

We decided to ask the "spirit" of the Ouija board for its own assessment of what it is. Specifically, we wanted to know if the answers were coming from our unconscious minds or from the spirit world. Here's what we were told by an entity identifying herself as Genie, possibly a takeoff of the Genie from Aladdin's lamp.

"I am both a separate entity and the combination of your unconscious minds. I don't speak to you, except through the board. I'm not hanging around making stuff fall from shelves to get your attention. I'm part of a group of spirits . . . and so are you, though your awareness is focused in the physical world."

We asked one more question. *Why are so many people, including some mediums, afraid of Ouija boards?* "People fear it because of the perceived link to Satanic contact. That belief grew out of Christian dogma and the fear can attract lower entities."

If you're wary about spirit contact through a Ouija board, how about tuning into the spirit world through a radio or a recorder?

Electronic Voice Phenomena

It seems appropriate that in our high-tech world, we would make use of technical wonders of communication to contact the other side. Electronic voice phenomena (EVP) involves the recording of mysterious voices that seem to come from beyond the grave. These human-sounding voices are heard on audio and video recorders. Usually, the voices are heard after they've been recorded and replayed at a high volume. The theory behind the phenomenon is that spirits can utilize the electrical energy in a recording device to implant a message.

Thomas Edison, the inventor of the electric light bulb, had another bright idea. He not only professed a belief in the spirit world, he attempted to create a device for contacting the dead.

In 1920, Edison wrote in an essay, "If our personality survives, then it is strictly logical or scientific to assume that it retains memory, intellect, other faculties, and knowledge that we acquire on this Earth. Therefore . . . if we can evolve an instrument so delicate as to be affected by our personality as it survives in the next life, such an instrument, when made available, ought to record something."

However, it was more than three decades later that EVP came into existence, when two researchers, Swedish film producer Friedrich Juergenson and Latvian psychologist Konstantin Raudive, independently began compiling recordings of what they claimed were voices from the other side. They believed that spirits were able to interact with the magnetic particles on recording tape, providing a record of their communication and proof of life after death. Today, numerous researchers continue experimenting and collecting these mysterious recordings.

Interpretations of such recordings can be subjective. A skeptic might not hear what seems clear to the believer.

Spirit Music

Here's an example of an unusual recording related to a departing soul. In this particular incident, described by Connie Cannon of St. Augustine, astonished family members recorded "spirit music" as they waited in a vigil for the death of a relative.

"Several family members, including myself, watched and listened to 'invisible fingers' playing my mother's piano in her home when she was in her final coma miles away in the hospital. We taped it, and got a credible, documented EVP." Connie, a medium, added, "It's been my experience that some spirits who were extremely powerful in physical vehicles have those energies magnified tremendously when the cocoon of skin is dropped and can manifest accordingly."

How to Make EVP Recordings

All you need is a cassette tape or digital recorder, preferably one that allows you to plug in an external microphone. If you're using a cassette tape, make sure it's a high bias tape.

There are two methods for making the recordings. The direct method involves simply turning on the recorder in a quiet place and recording for several minutes. Make sure there are no disturbances, such as road traffic sounds or voices from another room. The other method involves tuning a radio between stations and recording the white noise, but make sure that you're not picking up a faint station.

When you turn on the recorder, say the date, time, and location. You might announce that you would like to record a message from a spirit guide. You could also ask a specific question or ask the name of the speaker. Maintain a serious and respectful attitude throughout the session. Don't try cajoling the spirits or joke about what you're doing.

Record for several minutes, then rewind and play back your recording with the volume turned up. If you hear a voice say a word or phrase, note the location by the counter number on the recorder. Make sure it didn't come from an external source, such as someone arriving in another room.

If you don't succeed on your first attempt, try a different time and location. Graveyards are a popular choice for making EVP recordings. Keep a journal describing your efforts and your successes. Be specific and detailed. Is the word or phrase spoken clearly or is it muddled? Is it loud or a whisper? Was it a response to a question? Did you recognize the voice?

If you're successful, play the recording for people who weren't present and see if they hear the same words. Follow up with more questions at another session.

In the Spirit

Whether you're using electronic gadgets, a Ouija board, or automatic writing, these tools can be bypassed as you deepen a meditation practice or become more aware of your dreams. Sometimes, when you find yourself in a heightened state of awareness, especially through trying circumstances that you can't control, you can make such contact through synchronicity. You might be praying or pleading for help or resolution when the answer comes in a very unusual way.

Such was the case in 2004, when a massive hurricane struck our area. Frances, a sluggish, super-sized storm, covered 435 miles of the state, from Tallahassee to Key Largo, with wind and drenching rain. In some areas, the storm dumped nearly two feet of rain. By dark, our power was out, our yard was flooded, and the street in front of our house had turned into a river. Our front door and skylights were leaking. We sopped up what we could with towels, but feared that at some point our skylights might collapse. We moved everyone into the back bedroom—three humans, a dog, three cats, and a bird.

Around five in the morning, everyone was asleep except Trish, who just lay there, listening to the rain hammering the shutters and the skylights. Exhausted and frightened that the skylights wouldn't hold, she debated getting up and moving through the house again to check for leakage. Instead, she briefly shut her eyes—and suddenly "saw" a column of light shooting out from between her eyes and extending upward, through the ceiling. At the very top of this column, she could see beings peering over the edge, down at her, and heard soft murmurings, like voices.

She had seen this column of light and these beings, three of them, four years earlier, at a workshop with Eric Pearl, author of *The Reconnection*. They looked alien, but didn't feel the least bit hostile. If anything, they seemed merely curious about her, her world, and what was going on.

She felt an immediate reassurance that the house and everyone inside would make it through the storm just fine. With that, she fell asleep instantly. When she woke several hours later, Frances was finally moving on and the house had come through the deluge without major damage.

So what were these beings peering down at her through this column of light? To this day, Trish isn't sure. But the experience made her feel as if she and her family and home were somehow protected.

In whatever form they appear, spirit guides are waiting for you to make contact. But make sure that you're ready, that you're serious, that you're looking for guidance and not just playing games. Seek spirits of equal or higher vibration that will provide you with the help, the healing, the illumination you need. You might work through a credible medium, or you might encounter a spirit guide on your own. Whenever you make contact, give thanks for the guide's assistance and know that you are more than a physical being, that a part of you already exists on the other side.

CONCLUSION

Synchronicity is a multifaceted gem, and its beauty lies in what it teaches each of us about ourselves and the universe in which we live. Think of it as a kind of twilight zone of magic, the border where our inner and outer worlds meet. It's never something to be feared. In fact, the more frequently you experience it, the less fragmented you are as a human being and the more facets of that gem you'll perceive.

When synchronicity is combined with spirit contact, new realms of possibilities and potentials open. As the real-life stories in our book illustrate, our ideas about the nature of reality and our roles in this corner of the universe expand. We suddenly realize we are never alone, that consciousness cannot be annihilated, and that our loved ones are never really gone. They remain as close to us as a whisper, an invisible touch, a quick movement in the peripheral vision.

For each of us, our life's journey can be fraught with fear, suspicion, and hatred or with passionate curiosity, optimism, and faith that the universe is benevolent. Even when we experience a synchronicity that seems dark or cruel, we have the ability to look beyond the immediate and glimpse the larger picture, the underlying order beneath the chaos. By cracking synchronicity's symbolic code, we are invited into the mystery of the divine.

Appendix

RESOURCES

Bohm, David. *Wholeness and the Implicate Order*. London. Routledge Classics, 1980.

Brinkley, Dannion. *Saved by the Light*. New York. Harper One, 2008.

Bro, Harmon Hartzell. *A Seer Out of Season: The Life of Edgar Cayce*. New York. St. Martin's Paperbacks edition, 1996.

Broughton, Richard. *Parapsychology: The Controversial Science*. New York. Ballantine Books, 1991.

Chopra, Deepak. *The Spontaneous Fulfillment of Desire: Harnessing the Infinite Power of Coincidence*. New York. Harmony Books, 2003.

Combs, Allan and Mark Holland. *Synchronicity: Science, Myth, and the Trickster*. New York. Marlowe & Company, 1989.

Crichton, Michael. *Travels*. New York. Ballantine Books, 1988.

Crookes, William. "Notes of an Enquiry into the Phenomena called Spiritual during the Years 1870–1873." *Quarterly Journal of Science,* January 1874.

Dossey, Larry. *Reinventing Medicine*. San Francisco. Harper San Francisco, 1999.

Eden, Donna. *Energy Medicine: Balance Your Body's Energies for Optimum Health, Joy and Vitality*. New York. Jeremy P. Tarcher/Putnam, 1999.

Edward, John. *Crossing Over*. San Diego, California. Jodere Group, 2001.

Grasse, Ray. *The Waking Dream: Unlocking the Symbolic Language of Our Lives*. Wheaton, Illinois. Quest Books, 1996.

Guiley, Rosemary Ellen. *Dreamwork for the Soul: A Spiritual Guide to Dream Interpretation*. New York. Berkeley Books, 1998.

Heath, Pamela Rae and Jon Klimo. *Handbook to the Afterlife*. Berkeley, California. North Atlantic Books, 2010.

Hopcke, Robert. *There are No Accidents*. New York. Riverhead Books, 1997.

Ingerman, Sandra. *Shamanic Journeying: A Beginner's Guide*. Boulder, Colorado. Sounds True, 2004.

Jung, Carl. *Memories, Dreams, Reflections*. New York. Vintage, 1989.

Jung, Carl, editor. *Man and His Symbols*. New York. Dell Publishing, 1968.

Lanza, Robert and Bob Berman. *Biocentrism: How Life and the Universe Are the Keys to Understanding the True Nature of the Universe*. Dallas, Texas. BenBella Books, 2009.

MacGregor, Trish and Rob. *The 7 Secrets of Synchronicity*. Avon, Massachusetts. Adams Media, 2010.

MacGregor, Trish and Millie Gemondo. *Animal Totems: The Power and Prophecy of Your Animal Guides*. Gloucester, Massachusetts. Fair Winds Press, 2004.

Mansfield, Victor. *Synchronicity, Science, and Soul-Making*. Chicago. Open Court Publishing Company, 1995.

Martin, Joel and Patricia Romanowski. *Love Beyond Life: The Healing Power of After-Death Communications*. New York. HarperCollins Publishers, 1997.

McGuire, William and R. F. C. Hull, editors. *C. G. Jung Speaking: Interviews and Encounters*. Princeton, New Jersey. Princeton University Press, 1977.

Moss, Robert. *The Dreamer's Book of the Dead*. Rochester, Vermont. Destiny Book, 2005.

Owen, Iris M. with Margaret Sparrow. *Conjuring Up Philip*. New York. Pocket Books, 1977.

Peirce, Penney. *Frequency: the Power of Personal Vibration*. New York. Atria Books, 2009.

Roach, Mary. *Spook: Science Tackles the Afterlife*. New York. W.W. Norton & Company, 2005.

Roberts, Jane. *Seth Speaks*. San Rafael, California. Amber-Allen Publishing, 1972.

Rogan, Lisa. *Haunted Heart: The Life and Times of Stephen King*. New York. St. Martin's Press, 2008.

Sams, Jamie. *Dancing the Dream: The Seven Sacred Paths of Human Transformation*. San Francisco. Harper San Francisco, 1999.

Schulz, Mona Lisa. *Awakening Intuition: Using your Mind-Body Network for Insight and Healing*. New York. Random House, 1999.

Stemman, Roy. *Spirits and Spirit Worlds*. London. Aldus Books Limited, 1975.

Stuart, Nancy Rubin. *The Reluctant Spiritualist: The Life of Maggie Fox*. New York. Harcourt, Inc., 2005.

Talbot, Michael. *Beyond the Quantum: How the Secrets of the New Physics are Bridging the Chasm Between Science and Faith*. New York. Bantam Books, 1988.

Talbot, Michael. *The Holographic Universe*. New York. Harper Collins, 1991.

Weisberg, Barbara. *Talking to the Dead: Kate and Maggie Fox and the Rise of Spiritualism*. San Francisco. Harper San Francisco, 2004.

Wilson, Colin. *C.G. Jung: Lord of the Underworld*. London. Aeon Books Limited, 2005.

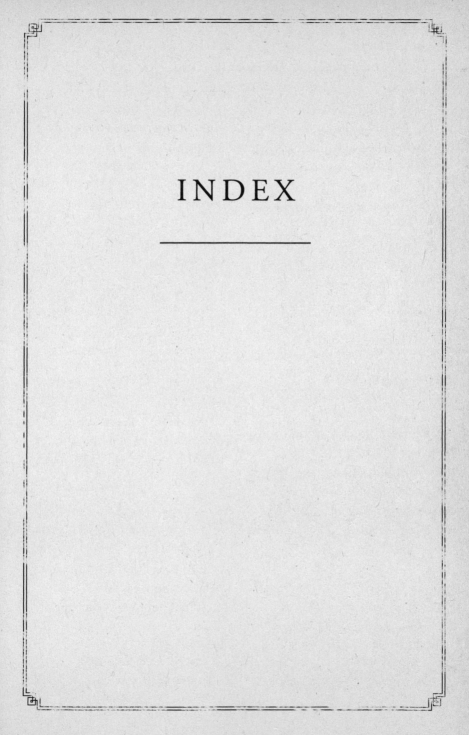

INDEX

ABOUT THE AUTHORS

Trish MacGregor and Rob MacGregor have been professional writers for twenty-six years. Their longtime interest in synchronicity led them to write *The 7 Secrets of Synchronicity* (Adams Media) in 2010. They've written books on dreams, psychic development, astrology, yoga, the tarot, divination, and animal symbolism. They've written the popular Sydney Omarr astrology series since 2003.

As novelists, both have won the prestigious Edgar Allan Poe Award: Trish for *Out of Sight*, and Rob for *Prophecy Rock*, a YA mystery. Its sequel, *Hawk Moon*, was an Edgar finalist. Rob also wrote *Indiana Jones and the Last Crusade* and six other original Indiana Jones novels. His novels *Time Catcher* and *Double Heart* will be published in the fall of 2011. Trish's most recent novel is *Esperanza* which will be followed by *Ghost Key*. Her works have been translated into thirteen languages. The MacGregors reside in South Florida.